GARDEN ILLUSIONS

· GARDENING · BY · DESIGN ·

GARDEN ILLUSIONS

· ALAN · TOOGOOD ·

Salem House Publishers
Topsfield, Massachusetts

ACKNOWLEDGEMENTS

The publishers are grateful to the author for granting permission to reproduce the colour photographs on pp 50 and 51. The photographs on pp 2, 10, 11, 18, 19, 22, 23, 26, 27, 30, 31, 34, 35, 38, 39, 42, 43, 46, 47, 59, 62, 63, 66, 67, 70, 71 and 75 were taken by John Heseltine. The murals depicted in the photographs on pp 26 and 27 were painted by Tim Plant. The garden shown on pp 22 and 39 was designed by Robin Williams; the gardens shown on pp 66 and 71 were designed by Myles Challis and David Stevens respectively.

All the line drawings were drawn by Nils Solberg.

© Ward Lock Limited 1988

First published in the United States by Salem House Publishers, 1988,
462 Boston Street, Topsfield, Massachusetts, 01983.

Library of Congress Cataloging in Publication Data:

Toogood, Alan S.
  Garden illusions.

  (Gardening by design)
  1. Gardens – Design. 2. Landscape gardening.
I. Title. II. Series.
SB473.T65   1988   712'.6   88-3165
ISBN 0-88162-330-X

CONTENTS

PREFACE

Here we have another unique title in the *Gardening by Design* series. I doubt if another book has ever been written on the subject of *Garden Illusions*.

But what exactly are garden illusions? The dictionary definition of illusion is: "the act of deceiving; that which deceives; a false show; a delusion; a deceptive sensuous impression" (Cassell's). Certainly in creating garden illusions we are endeavouring to deceive the eye.

Examples include making the garden appear larger than it really is by skilful design of such features as lawns; creating elements of surprise; the use of focal points, colours and sizes of plants; and even the use of carefully placed mirrors and murals.

We can also make very narrow gardens appear much wider, so you need never again feel as though you are living in a corridor.

We can completely blot out the surrounding 'landscape', such as large buildings and factory chimneys, in order to create a totally different atmosphere in the garden: perhaps with a view to turning it into a little bit of Mediterranean countryside, a cottage-style or Japanese-style garden, or even a 'tropical' jungle!

On the other hand, you might want to preserve a particularly pleasing view of the surrounding countryside, and indeed utilize it to make the garden appear to extend beyond the boundary and so appear very much larger than it really is.

Most gardens contain something which is decidedly unattractive and needs hiding. How many readers sit in their gardens looking at an oil-storage tank, a blank garage wall, a coal-bunker and even the dustbins? Quite a few, I imagine, but there are many attractive and ingenious ways of hiding such objects.

The majority of gardens, particularly small town and suburban plots, are perfectly flat, yet there is no need for them to appear so: again, deceive the eye with raised patios and borders; with steps that do not necessarily lead anywhere, except perhaps to a convincing wall mural; or with 'banks' of plants.

This book, then, is concerned with ideas and designs that deceive the eye. It also contains some practical tips on construction of features and planting techniques, which I hope you will find welcome.

I hope you enjoy the specially commissioned photographs and drawings and that they inspire you with some original and exciting ideas.

A.T.

1

BIG IDEAS

By today's standards a garden of a quarter of an acre is considered to be large, although it is by no means uncommon in older housing developments and estates. Owners of newer houses invariably have much smaller gardens. I hesitate to quote an average size, but perhaps would not be far out if I said that plots ranging from about $6 \times 12\,m$ ($20 \times 40\,ft$) to around $12\,m$ ($40\,ft$) square are the norm today.

Small gardens – and I am including all of the above examples in this category – need to be designed extremely carefully and most people will undoubtedly want to make them appear larger than they really are. There are certainly many ideas that could be used to achieve this effect, as will be revealed in this chapter.

CREATING A SENSE OF SPACE

There are various ways of creating a sense of space in a garden, particularly by the skilful design of the lawn (or paved area if a lawn is not a practical proposition) and ensuring that the entire garden cannot be seen in one glance.

Lawn shapes

Open space in the garden is usually provided by a lawn; or by a paved area if this is thought to be more practical in a small area. But whether lawn or paving, this open uncluttered part of the garden gives one a sense of space and room to stroll around.

The shape of the lawn will further help to create the illusion that the garden is more spacious than it really is. In a small square or rectangular garden avoid at all costs a lawn of similar shape but instead go for a lawn with gently curving or flowing edges (Fig. 1). Be as informal as you like with the design – the more irregular the better. Do not, however, make the curves too sharp or you may have difficulty with mowing.

There is absolutely no reason why similar informal shapes should not be created with paving materials – even pre-cast concrete slabs can be laid to an irregular design. With gravel it is even easier to create curving or flowing edges.

Elements of surprise

If the entire plot cannot be seen in one glance one gets the impression that the garden is larger than it really is. Therefore try to screen off a part, or several parts, of the garden to create some 'secret areas'. This is recommended even in the smallest garden, if possible.

There are various ways of screening parts of a garden and the least space-consuming way is to erect prefabricated timber trellis panels about $1.8\,m$ ($6\,ft$) high. This is an ideal method for very small gardens. Trellis does not drastically reduce light and neither does it create a claustrophobic effect, as could be the case with solid screens in a small area. Trellis, of

Fig. 1 In this small square plot the lawn shape creates the illusion of space. A disappearing stepping-stone path creates an element of surprise and two ornaments, acting as focal points, encourage one to explore.

course, provides yet another site for climbing plants.

There is available modern timber trellis in square or diamond pattern, or traditional trellis in more fancy designs.

A more substantial and certainly more expensive screen could be formed from screen-block walling. Large precast concrete blocks, with an openwork pattern, are used and one can go to a height of about 1.8 m (6 ft) provided supporting piers are used. Again, screen-block walling makes an excellent support for climbers and does not seriously reduce light.

Where there is more space available you might prefer a living screen, perhaps a formal hedge which can be kept quite narrow by regular clipping. Train it to a wedge shape – wider at the base than at the top. A formal hedge can be grown to a height of 1.8 m (6 ft) and ideally should be evergreen for year-round effect.

There are many plants suitable for formal hedges but bear in mind that some are slow-growing, particularly box *(Buxus sempervirens),* holly *(Ilex aquifolium),* and yew *(Taxus baccata).* Faster-growing hedging plants are Lawson's cypress *(Chamaecyparis lawsoniana)* varieties like 'Green Hedger', *Euonymus japonicus,* privet *(Ligustrum ovalifolium)* plus the golden variety 'Aureum', Portugal laurel *(Prunus lusitanica),* white cedar *(Thuja occidentalis),* and western red cedar *(Thuja plicata* 'Atrovirens').

If you prefer a less formal effect then consider instead groups of shrubs or conifers for screening parts of the garden. Of course, these will take up more space as they are left to grow naturally. However, some conifers have quite a narrow habit, forming cone or pillar shapes, such as *Juniperus virginiana* 'Skyrocket', *Chamaecyparis lawsoniana* 'Columnaris' and *C. l.* 'Green Pillar'. These eventually make quite tall specimens, as high as the average house, so I would only recommend them for larger plots, where they will not dominate the garden.

Groups of quick-growing shrubs which attain at least 1.8 m (6 ft) in height make attractive informal screens where sufficient space is available. Evergreens will give year-round screening and suitable kinds include: *Berberis darwinii,* a barberry with deep yellow flowers in spring; *Cotoneaster* 'Cornubia' with masses of red berries in autumn; *Stranvaesia davidiana,* which is rather like a cotoneaster, with heavy crops of crimson berries in autumn; *Viburnum tinus,* the laurustinus, with white flowers in winter and spring; and *Viburnum rhytidophyllum* with very attractive large leaves and creamy-white flowers in late spring.

A few deciduous shrubs planted among the evergreens will help to prevent a 'heavy' effect and I can recommend such kinds as *Forsythia* 'Lynwood' with yellow flowers in spring; the early-summer-flowering mock orange, *Philadelphus* 'Virginal'; the golden elder, *Sambucus nigra* 'Aurea', with yellow summer foliage; and, for autumn, a variety of guelder rose, *Viburnum opulus* 'Notcutt's Variety', with red berries and good autumn leaf colour.

Disappearing paths

Paths disappearing from view, say into the 'secret areas' (Fig. 1), also create an element of surprise and encourage one to explore. In my drawing I have shown stepping-stones (disappearing behind a group of shrubs) because in small gardens these do not dominate the scene, as solid paths can. Square, circular or hexagonal paving slabs can be used, setting them on well-firmed soil 15–22 cm (6–9in) apart, just below the surface of the lawn. Remember that paths should not be made too narrow – even in small gardens a minimum width should be 60 cm (2 ft).

Never make straight paths; instead curve them to give the impression of greater space in the garden. And make sure there is a feature at the end of each path – perhaps a secluded seat, a pool, or maybe a garden ornament.

DISTANCE AND DEPTH

When designing small gardens it is important to create a sense of distance and depth, again to make the garden

A path disappearing from view creates an element of surprise and encourages one to explore a garden.

This mirror really does create the illusion of extra depth by reflecting the trelliswork and water feature.

seem larger than it really is. There are many ways of achieving this, although it is unfortunate that some of the ideas are rarely considered by garden designers. This is a great pity for many gardens could benefit from some of the following suggestions, like the use of mirrors and murals to create the illusion of extra depth.

Vistas and focal points

A vista is simply a long view which creates a sense of distance. Every garden should have at least one vista, which could, for example, be from one corner of the garden to another; or it might be from a patio adjacent to the house to the far end of the lawn.

There must be something at the end of a vista to attract the eye and this is known as a focal point. A focal point encourages one to explore the garden. In my drawing (Fig. 1) I have included two focal points at the ends of long views. One has been placed at the curve in the stepping-stone path, so one is drawn to that area, whereupon we discover that the path leads into a secret area, hitherto hidden from view.

Focal points may be artificial or natural. In the former category one can include statuary, sundials, bird baths, ornamental garden seats and ornamental containers such as urns, pots and vases, perhaps on pedestals or plinths to give extra height. Remember that artificial focal points need a suitable background to show them off – for example, light-coloured statuary could have a dark shrub as a background.

Plants of distinctive shape can be used as focal points, such as pyramidal or cone-shaped conifers and plants with sword-like leaves such as yuccas and phormiums. Pale-coloured plants or objects will create a greater sense of distance than those of strong colours (see p. 15).

Focal points must be in scale with the garden. For example, very large objects or plants should not be considered for very small gardens as they would dominate the scene. Conversely, very small focal points in a large garden would be lost and fail to provide the desired effect of attracting the eye.

Creating illusions with plants

Planting schemes can be planned so that they create a sense of distance in the garden. One should consider such things as foliage size, colour and the arrangement of plants.

Foliage size

If large-leaved plants are grouped nearest the house and you gradually grade to small-leaved subjects at the far end of the garden, you will very effectively create a sense of distance: you will make the garden appear to be longer than it really is.

There is, of course, a vast range of plants that could be recommended, but the following lists comprise garden worthy, well known, large- and small-leaved shrubs.

LARGE-LEAVED SHRUBS

Aralia elata (Japanese angelica tree) A large shrub with massive deciduous compound leaves; can be pruned back if desired.

Aucuba japonica (spotted laurel) Evergreen, some varieties having gold-spotted leaves; height and spread 1.8 m (6 ft).

Clerodendrum bungei Deciduous rounded leaves, red flowers summer; height and spread 2.4 m (8 ft).

Datura suaveolens (angel's trumpet) Large deciduous shrub, huge white flowers; tender, so grow in tub and overwinter in greenhouse.

Eriobotrya japonica (loquat) Large evergreen shrub, white scented flowers.

Fatsia japonica Evergreen, large glossy hand-shaped leaves; height and spread 3.6 m (12 ft).

Ficus carica (fig) Deciduous, edible fruits; grow as a bush tree in tub, overwinter under glass.

Hydrangea villosa Large hairy deciduous leaves, mauve flowers; height and spread 2.4 m (8 ft).

Magnolia grandiflora 'Exmouth' Huge shiny evergreen leaves, massive cream flowers; best grown on sunny wall.

Mahonia japonica Compound evergreen leaves, yellow flowers winter and spring; height and spread at least 2.4 m (8 ft).

Paulownia tomentosa A large deciduous tree best grown as a shrub by cutting it back almost to ground level each year in early spring.

Prunus laurocerasus 'Magnoliifolia' (cherry laurel) Deep green shiny evergreen foliage; large shrub but can be pruned.

Rhododendron Where space permits, some rhododendrons have large, dramatic foliage, like *R. fictolacteum* and *R. falconeri*; need acid soil.

Rhus typhina (stag's horn sumach) Large compound leaves with good autumn colour; height and spread at least 3.6 m (12 ft).

Trachycarpus fortunei (Chusan palm) Large evergreen fronds, shaggy brown trunk; height and spread at least 2.4 m (8 ft).

Viburnum rhytidophyllum Deeply veined, shiny evergreen leaves, white flowers; height and spread 3.6 m (12 ft).

Vitis coignetiae Tall climber with massive leaves which take on brilliant tints in autumn.

Yucca gloriosa (Adam's needle) Erect sword-like leaves, evergreen; height and spread at least 1 m (3 ft).

LARGE-LEAVED PERENNIALS

Acanthus spinosus (bear's breeches) Prickly lobed leaves, spikes of purple and white flowers; height and spread 1 m (3 ft).

Bergenia (pig-squeak) Several species and varieties, with leathery evergreen leaves and pink, red or white flowers in spring; height and spread about 30 cm (12 in).

Beschorneria yuccoides Large, evergreen, sword-like leaves and reddish flower spike; height and spread at least 1 m (3 ft).

Cautleya robusta Large canna-like leaves give an exotic touch as do the spikes of yellow flowers; height at least 1 m (3 ft).

Crambe cordifolia Huge leaves and heads of white flowers; height up to 1.8 m (6 ft), spread 1 m (3 ft).

Eryngium *E. agavifolium* and *E. bromeliifolium* have long sword-like leaves and need plenty of space to develop.

Gunnera manicata A massive moisture-loving rhubarb-like perennial; height and spread 3 m (10 ft).

Helleborus Most of the hellebores have attractive, large, evergreen leaves and flower in winter or spring; height and spread 45–60 cm (18–24 in).

Hosta (plantain lily) Large choice of species and varieties in all shades of green, plus gold and variegated; height and spread 30–60 cm (12–24 in).

Kniphofia caulescens (red-hot poker) Broad grey grass-like foliage, spikes of light red flowers; 1.2 m (4 ft) high, spread 1 m (3 ft).

Ligularia clivorum 'Desdemona' Leaves purplish, 1.2 m (4 ft) spikes of orange flowers; spread about 60 cm (2 ft); needs moist soil.

Peltiphyllum peltatum (umbrella plant) Large umbrella-like leaves, pink flowers on tall stems; height at least 1 m (3 ft); moist soil.

Phormium (New Zealand flax) Evergreen sword-like leaves; many varieties ranging in height from 60 to 180 cm (2–6 ft).

Rheum palmatum 'Atropurpureum' (ornamental rhubarb) Purple-red leaves and 1.8 m (6 ft) spikes of cream flowers; spread 1 m (3 ft).

Rodgersia pinnata 'Superba' Bronze-purple foliage and pink flowers; height and spread 1 m (3 ft).

Veratrum nigrum Long ribbed leaves, spikes of deep purple flowers; height 1 m (3 ft), spread 45 cm (18 in).

Zantedeschia aethiopica 'Crowborough' (arum lily) Leaves arrow-shaped, large white lily-like flowers; height and spread up to 1 m (3 ft).

SMALL-LEAVED SHRUBS

Berberis thunbergii 'Kobold' (barberry) A dwarf ground-cover shrub with bright green deciduous foliage.

Buxus sempervirens 'Elegantissima' (box) Evergreen leaves with cream edges; height and spread about 1 m (3 ft) but growth is slow.

Cassinia fulvida Very tiny leaves, giving overall a

greeny-gold effect; height and spread to 1.5 m (5 ft).

Corokia cotoneaster (wire-netting bush) Congested mass of stems bearing tiny deep green leaves with white undersides; height and spread about 1.5 m (5 ft).

Cotoneaster Several of the cotoneasters have small foliage, like *C. microphyllus*, evergreen, red berries, height 15 cm (6 in), spread 1.8 m (6 ft); and *C. horizontalis*, deciduous, red berries, height 60 cm (2 ft), spread 1.8 m (6 ft).

Escallonia 'Edinensis' Partially evergreen, deep pink flowers; height and spread up to 3.6 m (12 ft).

Euonymus fortunei 'Kewensis' Prostrate ground-cover plant or climber, deep green leaves.

Hebe rakaiensis (shrubby veronica) Evergreen, light green foliage; height and spread up to 60 cm (2 ft).

Hedera helix 'Tres Coupe' (ivy) Green lobed leaves; use as climber or ground cover; slow grower.

Ilex crenata 'Golden Gem' (holly) Tiny evergreen golden leaves; height and spread about 45 cm (18 in).

Lonicera nitida (Chinese honeysuckle) Tiny evergreen leaves, vivid green in variety 'Elegant', up to 1.5 m (5 ft) in height and spread, and yellow in 'Baggesen's Gold', height and spread at least 1.8 m (6 ft).

Lonicera pileata Tiny evergreen leaves, vivid green; dwarf habit, used for ground cover.

Muehlenbeckia axillaris (wire-netting plant) Forms a congested mass of thin stems bearing tiny leaves; use for ground-cover or as climber.

Olearia × haastii (daisy bush) Evergreen, deep green leaves, white undersides; height and spread 2.4 m (8 ft).

Osmanthus delavayi Deep green evergreen foliage, white scented flowers; height and spread 2.4 m (8 ft).

Philadelphus microphyllus (mock orange) Deciduous foliage and small scented white flowers; height and spread up to 1 m (3 ft).

Prostanthera rotundifolia Tiny evergreen leaves and violet flowers, only for mild areas; height and spread up to 1.5 m (5 ft).

Rhododendron Some of the dwarf evergreen rhododendrons have tiny leaves, like *R. impeditum* and *R. scintillans*, with purplish-blue flowers. Lime-free soil needed.

Syringa microphylla 'Superba' (lilac) Small deciduous leaves and deep pink flowers; height and spread 1.8 m (6 ft).

SMALL-LEAVED PERENNIALS

Adiantum pedatum (maidenhair fern) A hardy fern with pinnate pale green fronds; height and spread about 45 cm (18 in).

Calamintha nepetoides Aromatic foliage and tiny lilac flowers; height 60 cm (2 ft).

Campanula poscharskyana (bellflower) Blue starry flowers set against small green leaves; height 30 cm (12 in), spread double this.

Lamium maculatum (dead nettle) Useful ground-cover plant in its varieties like 'Beacon Silver' with silvery foliage and 'Aureum' with golden leaves.

Melissa officinalis (lemon balm) Aromatic foliage, golden in variety 'Aureum'; height 75 cm (2½ ft).

Mentha (mint) Some of the mints are very ornamental, particularly gold-variegated *M. × gentilis* 'Variegata' and white-variegated *M. rotundifolia* 'Variegata'; height 45–60 cm (18–24 in).

Saxifraga umbrosa (London pride) Rounded evergreen leaves and clouds of pink flowers; height and spread 30 cm (18 in).

Thalictrum rocquebrunianum (meadow rue) Greyish pinnate leaves, sprays of pink flowers; height 1.2 m (4 ft), spread 60 cm (2 ft).

The use of colour

Colour can also be used to create a sense of distance. Pale-coloured plants, such as greys, silvers and those in pale shades of blue, mauve and green, which are not seen very clearly by the human eye, create a sense of distance and therefore could be planted at the far end of a garden. Strong-coloured plants, on the other hand, are seen more clearly and appear to be nearer the eye than those with pale colours. Therefore plants with strong colours – such as red, orange, crimson, scarlet, purple and deep blue, could be planted nearest the house.

Between these you could arrange plants which are neither very pale nor very dark, so that you achieve a gradation from dark to light down the length of the garden.

PALE-COLOURED SHRUBS

Buddleia (butterfly bush) *B. alternifolia* and *B. fallowiana* have respectively light green and grey deciduous foliage, and pale blue flowers; height and spread of former 6 m (20 ft), the latter half of this.

Caryopteris × clandonensis Greyish foliage and blue flowers, deciduous; height and spread up to 1.2 m (4 ft).

Chamaecyparis lawsoniana (Lawson cypress) Some of the larger-growing varieties have bluish-grey foliage, like 'Columnaris', 'Allumii' and 'Pembury Blue'.

Juniperus chinensis 'Pyramidalis' (Chinese juniper) A better conifer for the smaller garden, with greyish or bluish green foliage.

Lavandula spica (lavender) Light grey evergreen foliage, light grey-blue flowers; height and spread about 1 m (3 ft).

Perovskia atriplicifolia 'Blue Spire' Greyish green ferny deciduous foliage, spikes of grey-blue flowers; height about 1.2 m (4 ft).

Pinus strobus 'Nana' (dwarf Weymouth pine) Evergreen silvery blue-green foliage; height and spread 2.4 m (8 ft).

Pyrus salicifolia 'Pendula' (willow-leaved pear) Small weeping tree, silvery deciduous willow-like leaves; height and spread up to 6 m (20 ft).

Ruta graveolens 'Jackman's Blue' (rue) Evergreen greyish-blue ferny foliage; height and spread 45 cm (18 in).

Santolina neapolitana (cotton lavender) Evergreen feathery grey foliage; height and spread 60 cm (2 ft).

PALE-COLOURED PERENNIALS

Anaphalis yedoensis (pearl everlasting) Greyish leaves and white flowers; height and spread 60 by 30 cm (2 by 1 ft).

Artemisia 'Lambrook Silver' Has grey foliage, much divided, height 1 m (3 ft), and 'Powis Castle' has feathery silver leaves, height 60 cm (2 ft).

Campanula latifolia 'Gloaming' (bellflower) Greyish blue bell-shaped flowers in spikes; height 1 m (3 ft), spread 45 cm (18 in).

Echinops ritro (globe thistle) Greyish green foliage and steel blue globe-shaped flowers; height 1 m (3 ft), spread 60 cm (2 ft).

Eryngium maritimum (sea holly) Very pale green deeply divided leaves, steel-blue flowers; height and spread up to 45 cm (18 in).

Festuca glauca (fescue) Dwarf grass, 25 cm (10 in) high, with thin grey-blue leaves.

Helictotrichon sempervirens A dwarf grass with thin blue-grey leaves; height and spread 60 cm (2 ft).

Nepeta × faassenii (catmint) Greeny grey foliage and hazy blue flowers in spikes. Good variety is 'Six Hills Giant'; height and spread 60 cm (2 ft).

Veronica gentianoides (speedwell) Light blue flowers in spikes; height and spread 30 cm (12 in).

STRONG-COLOURED PLANTS

There are many of these to choose from and, among the shrubs, I suggest purple-leaved varieties of *Acer palmatum* (Japanese maple), berberis, *Corylus maxima* (filbert) and *Cotinus coggygria* (smoke bush). Deep blues can be obtained from varieties of ceanothus and hydrangea; while strong orange and red can be provided by the berrying pyracanthas and, on acid soils, by rhododendrons and azaleas.

Among the perennials strong orange and red shades can be found among crocosmias, *Euphorbia griffithii* 'Fireglow', *Lychnis chalcedonica, Monarda didyma, Paeonia lactiflora, Papaver orientale* (oriental poppy) and *Phlox paniculata* (border phlox). Deep blues and purples will be found among varieties of border delphinium and *Salvia superba*.

Fig. 2 To create the illusion of extra depth in planting schemes, plants can be staggered so that not all can be seen in one glance. Some groups can be brought well forward and other groups set well back.

Staggering plants

To create the illusion of extra depth in planting schemes, plants can be staggered so that not all can be seen in one glance (Fig. 2). For instance, in a border running down the length of the garden some groups of plants can be bought well forward and other groups set well back. To make this easier, one could have a border of very irregular outline (see drawing).

Camouflaging boundaries

Very dense planting, using shrubs and climbing plants, can completely hide boundary walls and fences and will help to give the impression of extra depth. It will also give the feeling that the garden extends beyond the boundaries. You will feel that you can walk through this dense growth and find more garden beyond.

In addition, dense planting can be used to shut out views beyond the garden, such as streets and other houses, again creating a sense of extra depth.

In some situations, such as very tiny backyards or courtyards, it might be more practical to use potted plants to create this impression of depth, arranging them on tiered timber staging against a wall to elevate them to a suitable height. Collections of trailing plants, for example, could be pot grown to provide a 'curtain' of foliage, like varieties of small-leaved ivy *(Hedera helix)*, periwinkles (vincas) and yellow archangel *(Lamiastrum luteum* 'Variegatum') with its silver-splashed leaves. The cascading foliage will, of course, hide the pots.

Creating illusions with mirrors

In garden design very little use is made of mirrors mounted on walls, which is a pity for they really do help to create the impression of extra depth by reflecting part of the garden. It can appear that the garden extends beyond the wall, particularly if the mirror is suitably framed.

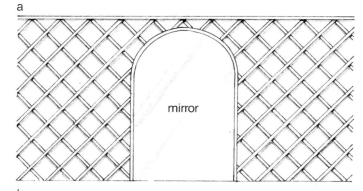

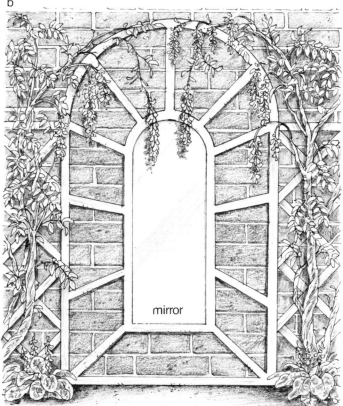

Fig. 3 *(a)* This mirror has been framed with trellis to give the illusion that one is looking through an archway.
(b) False-perspective trellis surrounding a mirror creates the illusion of an arched path. Note that climbing plants are allowed to partially hang down in front of the mirror.

A disappearing path tempts one to explore this well–planted and secluded garden. Gravel is an economical material for paths.

Seats have been used as focal points to attract the eye, wherever this meandering path changes direction.

Mirrors are also useful in dark areas because they reflect light; and at night they can be illuminated with garden lighting.

It is essential, outdoors, to use heavy plate-glass mirrors, which are best mounted on brick walls. You must order a mirror with a waterproof back, or seal it yourself to protect it from the weather by applying two or three coats of red oxide bitumastic paint. Additionally, seal the edges with bitumastic tape to stop water from penetrating.

Indoors the normal way of fixing a mirror to a wall is by means of brass screws inserted through holes pre-drilled in the mirror, suitably buffered with special plastic or rubber washers. This system can be used outdoors, but the screw heads rather spoil the illusion and so should be hidden by the surrounding framework. Alternatively, you may be able to make a suitable framework to hold the mirror, securing this to the wall rather than the mirror itself.

Of course, a mirror simply mounted in isolation on a wall does not create the effect we desire. It must be suitably framed so as to create the illusion that we are, for instance, looking through an arch or some other opening in the wall. An archway can be created with trellis mounted on the wall, as shown in Fig. 3a. Or you could use false-perspective trellis to create the illusion of an arched path (see Fig. 3b). False-perspective trellis units of this type are supplied by some garden centres in the UK; but if you fail to find a supplier then it is a fairly simple matter to make your own, using thin wooden laths. The arched top could be cut out of a sheet of plywood. The false-perspective trellis can be flanked on either side by normal ready-made trellis panels.

The trellis should be screwed to the wall but held about 2.5 cm (1 in) away from it with suitable spacers (old cotton reels, for instance, make ideal spacers).

Another idea is to have a path leading right up to a wall and to erect a timber pergola over it, again right up to the wall (see Fig. 4). A mirror completely fills the rectangle formed by the end of the pergola and gives the illusion that the path and pergola continue.

Trelliswork and pergolas should be used as supports

Fig. 4 A path and timber pergola lead right up to a wall. A mirror completely fills the rectangle formed by the end of the pergola and gives the illusion that the path and pergola continue.

Fig. 5 A mural should be suitably framed to give the impression of a view as seen through a gap in a wall. This mural is framed with a false door frame, on which hangs an old-fashioned heavy timber door.

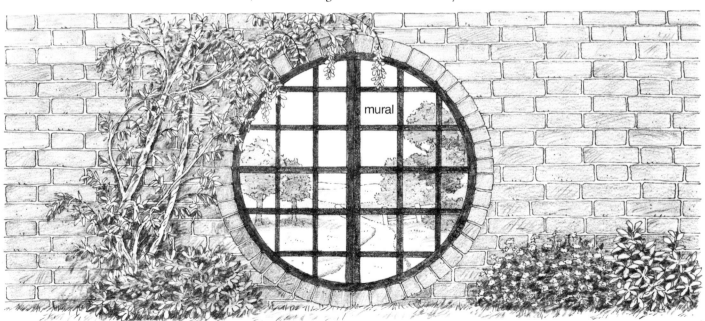

Fig. 6 A mural behind a wrought-iron gate can be very effective and convincing. Here a circular moon gate has been used. The circular course of bricks could be part of the mural.

The informal curving shape of this patio helps to create the illusion that the garden is more spacious.

An elaborate church-like summerhouse acts as a focal point at the end of this gently flowing lawn.

for climbing plants which can be allowed to hang down partially in front of the mirror. Indeed the use of plants immediately around a mirror is important for they are reflected and so help to create the illusion of greater depth.

Creating illusions with murals

Murals, or paintings on walls, serve a similar purpose to mirrors. Like mirrors they are not often used in gardens; but then let's face it, you would have to be a pretty good artist, for a mural must be as life-like as possible (perhaps a garden scene or a country view). Impressionist paintings are definitely not on in the garden situation! If you are not an artist, you may have a friend who is, and who might relish having a go at a mural.

Again a brick wall should be used, but of course the surface must be perfectly smooth and, if necessary, should be rendered with mortar. This is a skill in itself and you may require the assistance of a builder or plasterer. If the wall is already rendered, then check the condition of the rendering before making a start on the mural, and make repairs if necessary. It is absolutely essential that the wall is internally dry, with no rising damp. This should not be a problem if it is a house or garage wall, which should have a damp-proof course.

The area for the mural should be painted with white masonry paint, but not the type which contains fine sand as this gives a rather sandpaper-like texture which may be difficult to paint on. Before applying the masonry paint, treat the wall with stabilizing solution (masonry type) as this gives a hard, dust-free surface when dry, that does not allow the paint to soak into the wall.

Acrylic paints are used for the mural (the type used by artists). They are mixed with water, are quick drying, and then completely waterproof.

When the mural is complete you will need to seal it, so apply two coats of acrylic varnish (again, the type used by artists).

As with a mirror, a mural must be suitably framed to give the impression of a view as seen through a gap in a wall. For instance, a 'stone arch' could be painted around the scene. Or the mural could be framed with a false door frame (made of timber and fixed to the wall). You could even hang a real door on this (leaving it open, of course). A good choice for a country garden would be one of those old-fashioned heavy timber doors (Fig. 5).

A mural behind a wrought-iron gate can be very effective. Why not consider a circular moon gate as shown in Fig. 6? The circular course of bricks could, of course, be part of the mural.

Ideally the mural should be in keeping with the garden or locality, although there are examples in the UK of 'exotic locations' in small town and city gardens.

It could be a garden scene, in the same style as the real garden: perhaps with a central path disappearing into the distance, flanked by colourful plants, with a focal point such as a statue, urn or small temple at the end, and not forgetting to include sky. Or you may prefer a country scene, such as groups of trees with hills in the distance.

Plants should be planted right up to the mural to help give the impression that the garden continues beyond the wall. As with mirrors, you may also like to fix trellis around the mural for climbing plants, allowing them to partially hang over the mural.

A mural can also be enjoyed at night by spotlighting it with garden lighting.

2

A SENSE OF WIDTH

Many gardens are long and narrow, rather like corridors, and are typical of older, suburban and town houses. There are several ideas that could be put into practice to make these gardens appear wider than they really are.

DIAGONAL DESIGNS

If you are starting from scratch, or wish to completely re-design the garden, then consider the diagonal approach when drawing your plans so that the eye is taken across the plot, and indeed movement is from side to side, rather than down the length of the garden.

For instance, you could have a diagonal lawn, as shown in Fig. 7. To keep this garden as informal as possible I have designed a serpentine lawn, but note that it curves from one side of the garden to the other. Focal points have been carefully positioned to draw the eye from one side of the garden to the other: from the patio an ornamental garden seat is clearly visible; from the seat can be seen a statue on the other side of the garden; and from the statue a summerhouse in the far corner tempts one to that part of the garden. So one actually moves in a zig-zag pattern in this garden. Note that the boundaries have been densely planted to give the illusion of greater depth and that the entire garden cannot be seen in one glance from the patio, due to the fact that tall plants have been brought towards the centre of the garden to hide parts of it.

There are many other ideas for diagonal designs. For instance, a path zig-zagging across the plot will also give the illusion of greater width and would automatically divide the garden into a number of different areas, some of which could be screened with plants or artificial screens like trellis or screen-block walling.

USING CIRCLES

Using circles in designing a long narrow garden will also give a sense of greater width, as shown in Fig. 8. Here I have made use of interlocking circles, starting with a circular patio adjacent to the house. This could easily be formed of gravel if desired; alternatively a circular brick patio would be most attractive.

The lawn comprises two interlocking circles and would look attractive if edged with bricks. Again focal points have been carefully sited to draw the eye from one side of the garden to the other: note the two statues, and the specimen tree in a far corner. Towards the centre of this garden, some tall plants have been arranged to help create a surprise element.

If desired, circular beds could be included with the lawn and patio. Of course, the patio does not necessarily have to be adjacent to the house: one of the other circles, further down the garden, could be made into a sitting area, particularly if that is a sunnier part of the garden.

Any number of circles can be used: it all depends on the length of the garden. However, make maximum

A mural serves a similar purpose to a mirror. This view of the Taj Mahal is in a London garden.

Without this realistic mural the owners of the house would be staring at a brick wall.

Fig. 7 The diagonal approach has been used in the design of this long narrow garden so that the eye is taken across the plot. The serpentine lawn curves from one side to the other and focal points have been carefully positioned to draw the eye.

use of the width available to create the desired effect (nothing will be achieved by a series of small circles set in the centre of the plot).

MIRROR IMAGES

This is nothing to do with using mirrors to create illusions, but rather the use of pairs of plants or objects to help create the impression of greater width. This technique is shown in Fig. 9. The plants or objects must be identical and are arranged in pairs, one on each side of the garden, ideally as near as possible to the boundaries. Several such pairs can be used down the length of the garden.

Man-made objects which could be used include ornamental containers like urns, vases, pots and tubs. Each should be planted with the same kinds of plants, arranged in exactly the same way.

Twin statues might also be appropriate, together with bird-baths and ornamental garden seats.

Plants must be chosen very carefully – they must be distinctive kinds if they are to be used as specimens.

Fig. 8 Using circles in designing a long narrow garden will give a sense of greater width. These circles interlock. Focal points have been carefully sited to draw the eye from one side of the garden to the other.

There are quite a few ornamental trees, shrubs and conifers which are highly suitable, including some very slim or fastigiate kinds which would be suitable for very narrow gardens.

Let us firstly take a look at some very slim plants which would be suitable for limited space.

ULTRA-SLIM PLANTS

Berberis (barberry) Several of the berberis have a very slim habit of growth and therefore are well worth considering where space is limited. They are all *B.*

thunbergii varieties and are deciduous. 'Helmond Pillar' is very narrow and upright with deep purple foliage. It will attain a height of about 1.2 m (4 ft). Attaining a similar height are 'Red Chief' with striking leaves the colour of red wine, and 'Red Pillar' with deep red-purple foliage.

Juniperus virginiana 'Skyrocket' (juniper) This is a highly popular pencil-thin conifer suitable for the smallest gardens. It is quite a tall grower, though: within 10 years one can expect a height of about 2 m (6 ft), the ultimate height being around 6–7 m

Here a circular brick patio creates a sense of greater width in this rather narrow town garden.

A circular lawn, perhaps edged with stepping stones, is a good shape for a narrow garden.

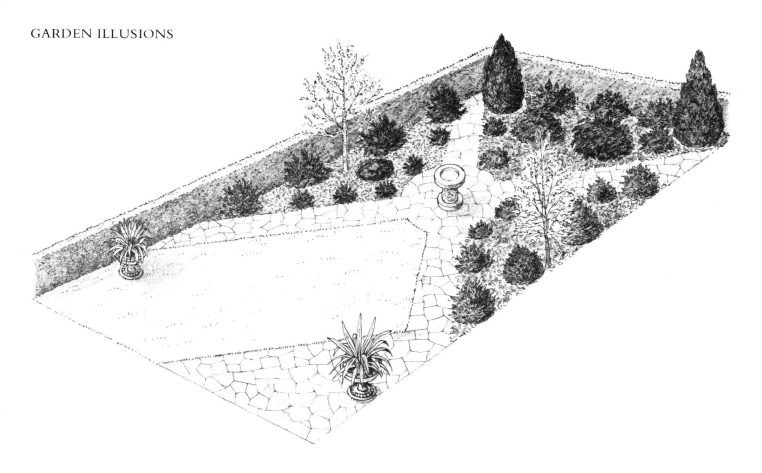

Fig. 9 A long narrow garden featuring mirror images and diagonal paths. The use of pairs of identical plants or objects creates the impression of greater width in a narrow plot. Distinctive trees or conifers are often paired up, as are ornamental containers and statues.

(20–23 ft). The foliage is bluish–grey, ideal for creating the impression of distance.

Prunus 'Amanogawa' (Japanese cherry) Most people like the spring-flowering Japanese cherries and this one is particularly suitable where space is very limited. It is completely upright and very slim, being wreathed in mid-spring with palest pink, semi-double flowers which are scented. It will grow to a height of at least 4.5 m (15 ft).

Taxus baccata 'Fastigiata' (Irish yew) Another popular conifer for small gardens, with dense, deep green foliage. It will eventually reach a height of about 4.5 m (15 ft). Even more attractive is the golden Irish yew, *T. b.* 'Fastigiata Aurea', with yellow-green foliage. The most intense colour is found in the young growth which is produced during the spring and early summer. This variety should be sited in full sun for the best foliage colour. It reaches a similar height to 'Fastigiata' but bear in mind that both are relatively slow-growing. Expect a height of about 2 m (6 ft) to be achieved in 10 years.

OTHER PLANTS FOR TWINNING

Where there is more space available, the following plants can be recommended for creating mirror images.

Acer palmatum (Japanese maple) The varieties of *Acer palmatum* are very distinctive plants and many are noted for their superb autumn leaf colour. All are deciduous. The smallest growers, with a height and spread of not more than 1.5 m (5 ft) include *A. p.* 'Dissectum' with ferny foliage and brilliant autumn colour; *A. p.* 'Dissectum Atropurpureum' with reddish-purple foliage, very deeply cut; and *A. p.* 'Dissectum Nigrum', also with ferny foliage which is purple-red in colour. A larger grower, with a height and spread of up to 3 m (10 ft) is *A. p.* 'Atropurpureum' whose lobed leaves are rich purple but become flushed with red in autumn. Larger still is *A. p.* 'Heptalobum Osakazuki' which grows over 3 m (10 ft) in height and width. It has plain green leaves which take on brilliant fiery tints in the autumn. The Japanese maples are best sited where they are protected from cold winds.

Chamaecyparis lawsoniana (Lawson cypress) The varieties described below are cone-shaped conifers, ideal for use as specimens. 'Ellwoodii' is a very popular variety with dense, grey-green foliage. In the winter it turns bluish. Eventual height is 4.5–6 m (15–20 ft), with a spread of 1.8–2.4 m (6–8 ft). Useful for creating a sense of distance is 'Fletcheri' with soft, grey-green foliage. It grows to a height of 5–7 m (16–23 ft), with a spread of 1.8–2.4 m (6–8 ft). 'Green Pillar' has erect layers of bright green foliage of outstanding texture. Eventual height is 10–12 m (33–40 ft), with a spread of 3 m (10 ft). The ever-popular 'Lanei' has golden foliage all year round. It needs plenty of sun. Eventual height is 10–15 m (33–50 ft), with a spread of 5 m (16 ft).

Cortaderia selloana (pampas grass) A very popular, large ornamental grass of distinctive appearance. The foliage is evergreen, greyish green in colour and sprays outwards like a fountain. The tall flower stems carry bold plumes of silvery white flowers in late summer and autumn. The variety 'Sunningdale Silver' has larger flowers than the species and is highly recommended. Height of both is at least 2.4 m (8 ft) when in flower, and spread 1.8 m (6 ft) or more. Pampas grass grows best if conditions are sunny and sheltered.

Corylus avellana 'Contorta' (corkscrew hazel) This is a most unusual shrub with twisted and curled stems and shoots. It shows up best in the winter when the leaves have fallen, and produces yellow catkins in late winter/early spring on the bare branches. It grows more slowly than the species but eventually makes a specimen up to 3 m (10 ft) in height with a spread of about 1.8 m (6 ft).

Malus tschonoskii (crab apple) This is a superb small tree of upright habit with a cone-shaped head of branches. It is of moderate interest in the spring when it bears its white blossoms, lightly flushed with pink. These are followed by red fruits but the tree really comes into its own in the autumn when the leaves take on spectacular crimson and gold tints.

Miscanthus (ornamental grass) The larger-growing miscanthus make stately and distinctive specimen plants and are easily grown in a sunny spot with well-drained soil. The largest is *M. sacchariflorus* which can reach a height of 3 m (10 ft) – this is annual growth, as the stems die down in autumn! The green leaves arch outwards and the overall spread of this grass is approximately 1 m (3 ft). There are two *M. sinensis* varieties which are also well worth growing. One is the purple-flushed *M. s. purpureus* and the other gold-banded *M. s.* 'Zebrinus', popularly called the zebra grass. Both of these will attain a height of about 1.5 m (5 ft) and have a spread of at least 60 cm (2 ft).

Phormium tenax (New Zealand flax) The phormiums are 'architectural' plants with bold, evergreen, sword-shaped leaves, ideal for formal situations. *P. tenax* itself has plain green leaves and can reach a height of 2.4 m (8 ft)), with a spread of about half of this. Varieties of similar size include 'Purpureum' with light purple foliage, and the green and cream striped 'Variegatum'. Phormiums are on the tender side and therefore not suited to cold parts of the country. A severe winter can kill them even in more

This boundary is well screened with a dense planting of large shrubs and small ornamental trees.

Very dense plantings of shrubs and climbers to hide boundary walls create the feeling of extra depth in a garden.

mild areas, so it pays to protect plants with straw in the winter. Moist yet well-drained soil and full sun are essential for their well-being.

Robinia pseudoacacia 'Frisia' (false acacia) This is a very popular small tree generally used as a specimen and it looks particularly well in a more formal garden. It is deciduous, with pinnate foliage, which starts off in spring as a very intense, deep yellow and fades during the summer to light yellow-green. It is a somewhat round-headed tree and eventually attains a height of at least 9 m (30 ft) with a spread of about two-thirds of this. It should be grown in full sun for the best leaf colour and needs a well-drained soil.

Sorbus aucuparia 'Fastigiata' (mountain ash) The ordinary mountain ash, *S. aucuparia*, is a popular small tree with a wide, rounded head of branches, which is quite space-consuming. However, the variety 'Fastigiata' has perfectly upright branches which form a narrow column, much more suitable for limited space. Height is up to 9 m (30 ft) and the spread in the region of 1–1.2 m (3–4 ft). The pinnate leaves are deep green and make an excellent background for the crop of large red berries which is a feature in the autumn. It is a good town tree but not recommended for very shallow chalky soils.

Yucca Like the phormiums, the yuccas are stately 'architectural' plants, ideal for formal gardens. They are all evergreen, with sword-shaped leaves, and produce spikes of white or cream lily-like flowers in the summer once they are well established. They need plenty of sun and well-drained soil. Of the popular species, I can recommend *Y. filamentosa*, popularly called Adam's needle, with greyish-green leaves. Height and spread about 1 m (3 ft), but the flower stem may reach double this. *Y. gloriosa* carries a rosette of deep green leaves on a woody trunk-like stem. The height and spread of this species are variable and can range from 1–2 m (3–6 ft). The flower stem may reach a height of 2 m (6 ft) also. You will have to be patient for this one to flower for it needs at least five years to settle down. Not unlike the last-mentioned, *Y. recurvifolia* has thinner leaves which splay outwards like a fountain. A similar size to *Y. gloriosa* and, like that species, it does not flower until very well established.

3

SCREENS AND VIEWS

The view beyond the garden will determine exactly how much screening is needed around the boundaries. Ugly views all round, such as created by many buildings, industrial sites and the like, may well make you decide that complete screening is needed if one is to create a different atmosphere around the house. For instance, if you want to create a country- or cottage-style garden in a city or town plot, then it does not help if you have a background of factory chimneys or a power station!

On the other hand, you may well have a pleasant view from your garden, perhaps of the countryside if you live in a rural or semi-rural area. This should be preserved and even utilized to make the garden appear larger – by skilful planning it is often possible to make the garden appear to extend beyond the boundary.

TALL SCREENS

Tall screens, either living or artificial, are needed to hide fairly large objects beyond the boundaries of the garden. I have already described some artificial screening materials (trellis and screen-block walling) in Chapter 1; and also in that chapter a range of hedging plants and large quick-growing shrubs suitable for screening. Any of these could be used for boundary screens.

However, when it comes to small gardens, there can be more of a problem in screening large objects. A boundary screen would have to be so tall that it would completely dominate the garden. A 1.8 m (6 ft) high hedge, group of shrubs or artificial screen will only partially hide the view; yet this is the most practical proposition for a small garden. The use of very tall living screens is only feasible in large gardens.

However, it is possible to completely hide a large building or some other object even in the limited space of a small garden. It is a case of positioning the screen in a suitable part of the garden. A tree is one of the most useful forms of partial screening in a small garden. Sometimes a single tree may be all that is needed to obscure a large building, provided it is planted in a suitable position. All too often people plant a tree far too close to the object they want to hide. The tree will therefore never effectively blot out the eyesore. Instead, the tree should be placed further away from the object, perhaps nearer the house or patio (see Fig. 10). Certainly, you will still be able to see the object when you walk beyond the tree, but at least it will not be visible from your house or patio. At the same time, one must be realistic and not plant a tree too close to the house, otherwise its roots may damage drains and foundations and it could drastically reduce the amount of light in the house.

The same technique can be used with groups of tall shrubs, hedges and artificial screens, of course.

For a small garden one should not choose a huge forest-type tree for hiding an unsightly object as it would completely dominate the garden. A small ornamental tree is all that is needed. The ideal tree would be evergreen, so that it remains effective all the year round; but unfortunately there are no small

The view beyond this garden is attractively blotted out with trellis screens, which support hanging baskets.

Parts of a garden can be screened with timber trellis panels which, of course, make admirable supports for climbing plants.

Fig. 10a This tree has been planted too close to the large building to blot it out effectively when viewed from the house or patio.

Fig. 10b This is a much better position for the tree: when one looks out of the windows or sits on the patio the large building is completely hidden.

fast-growing evergreen trees, unless you opt for one of the cone-shaped conifers such as a Lawson cypress variety. But these are of narrow habit compared to many other small trees which have wide-spreading branches, forming a somewhat rounded head, which is better for screening. You could, of course, plant a group of cone-shaped conifers if you have sufficient space.

Attractive small round-headed deciduous trees

include: *Betula pendula* 'Youngii' (Young's weeping birch); varieties of *Crataegus oxyacantha* (thorns); *Crataegus prunifolia* (thorn); *Fagus sylvatica* 'Purpurea Pendula' (the weeping purple beech); laburnums (golden rain trees); malus (crabs) like *M. floribunda*, 'Golden Hornet', *M. hupehensis*, 'John Downie', 'Lemoinei', 'Profusion' and 'Red Sentinel'; the ornamental cherries and plums like *Prunus cerasifera* 'Pissardii' (the purple-leaved plum), *P. subhirtella* varieties, and most of the Japanese cherries; *Pyrus salicifolia* 'Pendula' (the willow-leaved pear); *Robinia pseudoacacia* 'Frisia'; and the sorbus or mountain ashes, like *S. aucuparia* and varieties, *S. cashmiriana*, *S. hupehensis*, 'Joseph Rock', and *S. vilmorinii*.

There is scope for very tall living screens on the boundary if you have a large garden, so let us now consider these.

There is a range of fast or reasonably fast-growing deciduous and evergreen trees that can be used, both coniferous and broad-leaved. They may be planted in a single line or, for a really wide screen, in a double row, but staggering the plants in the rows. The trees should be planted 1.8–2.4 m (6–8 ft) apart to give a quick effect, but bear in mind that in later years some thinning out may be needed.

Tall trees for screens

I will not attempt to give the eventual heights of the trees listed below, for this can vary according to climate and soil conditions. Instead I have quoted the heights that can be achieved, in good growing conditions, within 20 years. You can either use one subject to form the screen or, to create more interest, mix several different subjects; perhaps a combination of deciduous and evergreen. A totally evergreen screen can appear rather 'heavy' and sombre.

DECIDUOUS TREES

Larix decidua (European larch) Very conspicuous bright green leaves in spring, good autumn colour; takes exposure but not thin chalky soils; 15 m 50 ft).

Populus alba (white poplar) Foliage white on the underside, good autumn colour; excellent for wet conditions and coastal gardens; tremendous root spread so keep well away from buildings – at least 30 m (100 ft): (this applies to all poplars); 12 m (40 ft).

Populus canescens (grey poplar) Foliage greyish on the underside, good autumn colour; excellent for wet conditions and coastal gardens; 9–15 m (30–50 ft).

Populus tremula (aspen) Good autumn leaf colour; excellent for wet conditions and coastal gardens; 9 m (30 ft).

Quercus robur (English or common oak) The mid-green leaves are attractively lobed; not suitable for shallow soils but excellent in exposed situations; 3.6–5.5 m (12–18 ft).

Salix alba (white willow) The foliage is attractive as it is whitish on the underside; highly recommended for coastal gardens, exposed situations and moist or wet ground; 12 m (40 ft).

Salix caprea (goat willow) Noted for its catkins in the spring, which appear before the ovate leaves; highly recommended for coastal gardens, exposed situations and moist or wet ground; 6–7.6 m (20–25 ft).

Sorbus aria (whitebeam) The large elliptic leaves are grey above and have brilliant white undersides; they colour well in autumn; very adaptable – will tolerate exposed situations, coastal conditions, atmospheric pollution (particularly recommended for industrial areas) and very chalky soils; 6 m (20 ft).

Tilia cordata (small-leaved lime) Attractive dark green foliage which is lighter on the underside; excellent choice for exposed situations and tolerates atmospheric pollution (suitable for industrial areas); 9 m (30 ft).

EVERGREEN TREES

Chamaecyparis lawsoniana (Lawson cypress) The foliage is mid-green and carried in feathery sprays; adaptable but do not subject it to very cold exposed conditions; 12 m (40 ft).

× **Cupressocyparis leylandii** (Leyland cypress) A very fast grower with dark green foliage carried in feathery sprays; excellent for coastal conditions and alkaline soils; 15 m (50 ft).

Cupressus macrocarpa (Monterey cypress) Feathery foliage, vivid green, very attractive; it will only succeed in areas with a mild climate and is suitable for mild coastal gardens; quite a fast grower; 15 m (50 ft).

A tall steel-mesh screen, which makes an ideal support for climbing plants, can effectively hide ugly views.

A combination of trelliswork and large shrubs used to screen parts of a garden to create 'secret areas'.

Picea abies (Norway spruce) Popular as a Christmas tree in the UK, but makes an excellent screen with its vivid green foliage; it will grow well in chalky soils and is very adaptable as regards climate; 15 m (50 ft).

Quercus ilex (evergreen oak) This excellent screening tree has very dark green, shiny foliage and is best planted with deciduous trees if a sombre effect is to be avoided; a popular choice for coastal gardens and it thrives in alkaline soils; 6 m (20 ft).

Thuja plicata (western red cedar) This conifer has vivid green, somewhat shiny leaves carried in feathery sprays; do not subject it to extreme exposure; best growth achieved in moisture-retentive soils but will grow reasonably well in thin alkaline soils; 15 m (50 ft).

PRESERVING PLEASANT VIEWS

Lucky is the garden owner who has a pleasant view from the garden – perhaps of the countryside or an attractive park. Such views should be preserved and indeed utilized to make the garden appear to extend beyond the boundary. By skilful planting and choice of plants one can often make the garden appear to be part of the surrounding country and consequently larger than it really is.

Firstly you should consider whether or not you want to define the boundary, say with a fence, wall or hedge. This will almost certainly be necessary if you have dogs or other pets which have to be kept under control; and indeed to keep small children within the garden. Ideally, to create the right effect one should not have a fence, wall or hedge but rather allow the garden to merge into the surroundings.

You must also consider whether or not it is an advantage to be able to see the entire view from the garden. Perhaps there are parts that are not so appealing. In this instance the most attractive part could be framed, say with a pair of trees, so that you create a vista. Then the remainder of the boundary could be defined with a hedge, wall or fence.

The part of the garden immediately behind this opening should be made to merge with the countryside beyond. This may mean, for instance, establishing a long-grass area which would make a home for many wild flowers, choosing those which are found naturally in the area. One can, of course, buy seeds of wild flowers – there are several suppliers. You may also be able to buy young plants of the kinds that you want to grow.

If you are in a heathland area then perhaps a heather garden would be more appropriate, ideally choosing species and natural varieties rather than hybrids. The highly-coloured foliage varieties, for instance, would look rather out of place here. A few dwarf pines planted here and there among the heathers would complete the picture.

If you live in the country it is important, I feel, to choose indigenous plants for the boundary which will help the garden blend much better into the surroundings. Find out which trees grow locally: they may be birches, pines, mountain ash, various acers, oak, beech or holly. Use appropriate trees to frame the view.

A country garden calls for a natural hedge, a haven for wildlife. It may be composed of several different subjects, such as the hawthorn or *Crataegus monogyna*; the field or hedge maple, *Acer campestre*; the guelder rose, *Viburnum opulus*; the elder, *Sambucus nigra*; or holly, *Ilex aquifolium*. It should be grown informally but may need judicious pruning to keep it reasonably neat. Over and through the hedge other wild plants can be allowed to grow, like the wild clematis, *C. vitalba*; the woodbine or honeysuckle, *Lonicera periclymenum*; the dog rose, *Rosa canina*; and even wild brambles and ivy. Again, find out which plants grow locally and use these. Wild flowers can be encouraged to grow at the base of the hedge.

4

OUT OF SIGHT, OUT OF MIND

In most gardens there is something which is decidedly unattractive and needs hiding. It may be a shed, garage, oil-storage tank, dustbins, coalbunkers, compost heap, tree stumps and old trees, man-holes and even the vegetable plot or prefabricated raised swimming pool. Here I consider ways of attractively hiding all of these objects to make the garden a more pleasant place for outdoor living.

TRELLIS CLADDING

Most garden sheds and garages are not considered to be the most attractive of buildings and therefore it is usually worthwhile trying to make them look as pleasing as possible.

It would be practical to partially enclose a small garden shed, as described under Enclosures on p. 52. The alternative is to clad sheds and garages with timber trellis and to grow climbing plants up and over them. Although not exactly an original idea it can, nevertheless, be very effective.

Prefabricated timber trellis panels are readily available in both square and diamond pattern. Some trellis is painted white by the manufacturer, which can look attractive in some situations, while other trellis available is in natural wood colours, such as western red cedar.

You may be able to cut and modify trellis panels to completely clad a shed, or it might be more practical to make your own from wooden laths (Fig. 11a).

Cladding a shed in this way raises the problem of how to carry out timber preservation of the shed in the future. One way around this is to fit hinges to the bottom of the trellis panels so that they can be gently lowered, or partially lowered, complete with plants. If carried out carefully this will not harm climbing plants as the stems are usually fairly supple.

A garage wall can be similarly clad and you could be even more adventurous and make quite a feature of it as shown in Fig. 11b. Here the entire wall has been clad with trellis, except for an 'archway' in which a mirror has been mounted to give an impression of depth and to reflect the pool and fountain in front of the wall. How much more attractive than a plain brick wall!

There is a very wide range of climbing plants that could be grown up and over the shed or garage, some being suitable for sun, others for shade. One or two are extremely fast-growing, ideal for quickly covering large buildings.

Climbers for sheds and garages

Actinidia kolomikta (kolomikta vine) Large green, white and pink deciduous leaves; needs sun and lime-free soil; height 3.6 m (12 ft).

Celastrus orbiculatus (staff vine) Deciduous; in autumn red and orange fruits and yellow foliage; sun or partial shade; very quick grower to 9 m (30 ft).

Chaenomeles speciosa (ornamental quince) Pink, red or white flowers in spring; deciduous; suitable for shade; height 1.8 m (6 ft).

An oil-storage tank well screened with shrubs, climbers and standard fuchsias, and painted an acceptable shade of green.

To create the feeling of warmth, use a red colour scheme, here created mainly with sedums and polygonums.

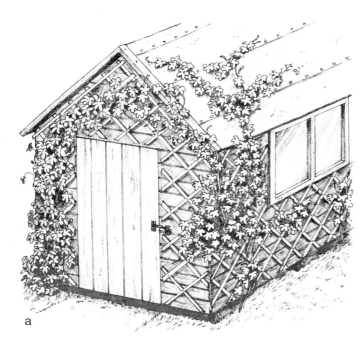

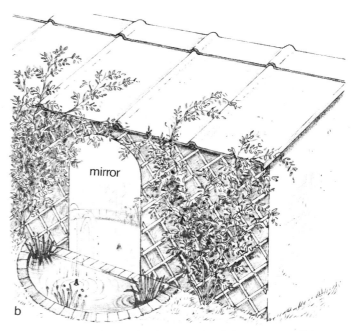

Fig. 11a This garden shed has been much improved by cladding it completely with timber trellis, which makes a support for climbing plants. These can be trained over the roof.

Fig. 11b Quite a feature has been made of this garage wall by cladding it with trellis and a mirror, and building a pool with a fountain in front of it.

Clematis (large-flowered clematis) Wide range available, with huge flowers mainly in summer; deciduous; needs sun; height around 3 m (10 ft).

Cotoneaster horizontalis (fishbone cotoneaster) Red berries in autumn; deciduous; suitable for shade; height 2.4 m (8 ft).

Humulus lupulus 'Aureus' (golden hop) Large, deep acid yellow leaves; herbaceous habit (stems die down in autumn); needs plenty of sun; height about 5 m (15 ft).

Hydrangea petiolaris (climbing hydrangea) White flowers carried in flat heads during summer; deciduous; suitable for shade; height 7.5 m (25 ft) plus.

Jasminum nudiflorum (winter-flowering jasmine) Masses of bright yellow flowers in winter; deciduous; suitable for shade; height at least 3 m (10 ft).

Jasminum officinale (common or summer jasmine) White, highly fragrant flowers in summer and early autumn; semi-evergreen; needs warm sunny spot; height 6 m (20 ft).

Lonicera periclymenum 'Belgica' (early Dutch honeysuckle) Yellow and red-purple fragrant flowers in early summer; deciduous; needs sun; height 6 m (20 ft).

Polygonum baldschuanicum (Russian vine) Masses of white flowers from mid–summer to early autumn; deciduous; sun or partial shade; a tremendously vigorous and quick-growing climber suitable for covering large buildings; height 12 m (40 ft).

Pyracantha (firethorn) The pyracanthas are laden with orange, red or yellow berries in autumn; evergreen; suitable for shade; height 3.6 m (12 ft).

Fig. 12a Pergolas can turn outbuildings or other objects into attractive features. This one has been erected alongside a garage and supports some attractive climbing plants.

Fig. 12b Here an oil-storage tank has been covered with a pergola, which has been made extra high for easy access to the tank. Again the pergola supports climbers.

Solanum crispum (Chilean potato tree) The purple-blue summer flowers are like those of the potato; semi-evergreen; needs plenty of sun and shelter; very vigorous, height 6 m (20 ft).

PERGOLAS

I consider that timber pergolas are extremely useful as they can turn a shed, garage or even an oil-storage tank into a highly attractive feature.

Pergolas can be obtained in kit form, which can be added to or extended as desired. But the DIY enthusiast should find it a comparatively simple matter to construct one from scratch, using sawn timber.

A pergola is essentially a support for climbing plants and some suitable kinds are described below.

A pergola could be erected alongside a garage or shed, using one of the walls to support one side of it, as shown in Fig. 12a. Sufficiently vigorous climbers should be able to grow right over the pergola and perhaps cover the shed or garage roof as well.

There is no reason why an oil-storage tank should not be covered with a pergola to turn it into a more attractive feature (Fig. 12b). However, do bear in mind that tanks are elevated and therefore overall they are quite high, necessitating a pergola which is much higher than normal. There must also be easy access to the top of the tank for filling so make sure there is plenty of headroom between it and the pergola. The oil-delivery man will not be too pleased if he bangs his

This is the famous red border at Hidcote Manor, Gloucestershire, featuring red roses and dahlias. It creates a 'warm' atmosphere.

A 'cool' colour scheme: the green and white garden at Hidcote Manor, featuring alchemilla and white campanulas.

head on timber beams! It would also be worth making sure that one or two of the front pillars are quickly removable, in case a tank replacement is required.

An alternative way of dealing with an oil-storage tank is to partially enclose it, as described under Enclosures on this page. Again, though, do make sure the tank is easily accessible for oil deliveries.

Climbers for pergolas

Laburnum (golden rain tree) No, this is not a climber but a tree. However, it can be trained over a pergola, when its trusses of yellow pea flowers will drip underneath in late spring and early summer. Suitable kinds for pergola training are *L. alpinum*, *L. anagyroides* and *L. × watereri* 'Vossii' which has ultra-long flower trusses. It is best to buy young bushes rather than trees as these will produce several stems. Tie in regularly the long shoots that are produced. In early winter each year cut back side shoots to within two or three buds. Full sun required.

Roses The modern repeat-flowering climbing roses, which produce several flushes of blooms during summer and autumn, are ideal for pergolas. There are lots of varieties to choose from, but some of my favourites include 'Aloha', coral pink, height 2.4 m (8 ft), suitable for shade; 'Altissimo', single red, height 4.5 m (15 ft); 'Danse du Feu', orange-red, suitable for shade, height 3 m (10 ft); 'Golden Showers', bright yellow, suitable for shade, height 2.4 m (8 ft); 'New Dawn', pale pink, suitable for shade, height 1.8 m (6 ft); 'Parkdirektor Riggers', single scarlet, height 2.4 m (8 ft); 'Pink Perpétue', bright pink, height 2.4 m (8 ft); and 'Swan Lake', white, height 2.4 m (8 ft). Note that some tolerate shade; the others need plenty of sun.

Vitis 'Brant' (grape vine) An ornamental vine with brilliant autumn leaf colour; the black grapes are edible; full sun; height 6 m (20 ft).

Wisteria floribunda 'Macrobotrys' (wisteria) One of the best wisterias, with extremely long trusses of lilac and blue flowers in spring and early summer; deciduous; full sun; height 5 m (15 ft).

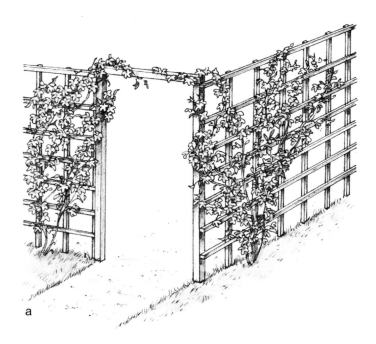

Fig. 13a One of the most economical ways of forming an enclosure for utility objects is to erect 1.8 m (6 ft) timber trellis panels. The entrance is formed with a pergola arch.

ENCLOSURES

Dustbins, coal-bunker, oil-storage tank, compost heap and other unsightly utility objects could be hidden in an enclosure. Perhaps this could be formed in a corner of the garden – wherever possible it makes sense to use existing boundary walls or fences. Then it is a case of putting up one or two more screens to form a 'compound' of suitable size.

One of the most economical ways of forming an enclosure is to erect 1.8 m (6 ft) high timber trellis panels as shown in Fig. 13a. The entrance could be formed with a pergola arch (available in kit form) to make it more attractive. One further word about entrances, though: bear in mind that tradesmen may

Fig. 13*b* A more ambitious enclosure can be formed with 1.8 m (6 ft) high screen-block walls. A further touch of elegance has been added by installing a wrought-iron gate.

have to use them, so there must be sufficient headroom and width to ensure easy movement of dustbins, sacks of coal and so on. If in doubt, dispense with the pergola arch and just have quite a wide opening in the screen.

As an alternative to trellis you may wish to use prefabricated timber fencing panels (the lapped or woven types) which are also quite economical.

More ambitious would be to build 1.8 m (6 ft) high screen-block walls, using pre-cast concrete blocks with an open-work pattern (Fig. 13b). A further touch of elegance could be added by installing a wrought-iron gate in the entrance.

If you make it sufficiently large an enclosure could well accommodate all your utility items – better than having them scattered all around the garden, necessitating several such structures.

Once again we now have some excellent supports for climbing plants and an enclosure should certainly be well clothed with a good selection. I have already described a range of climbers on pages 45, 48 and 52, so take your pick from these.

VEGETABLE PLOT

Do you consider the vegetable plot an attractive feature or an eyesore? I suppose it depends on how well you lay it out and maintain it. Some vegetable plots I have come across are aesthetically very pleasing, while others are nothing but 'weed-infested cabbage patches' which definitely need screening from the rest of the garden.

If you feel that you want to screen your vegetable plot then consider screens of trained fruits, which are both ornamental and highly productive.

A system of stout posts and horizontal wires, about 1.8 m (6 ft) high, could support a row of raspberries, or blackberries, loganberries and other hybrid berries.

A similar system of support could be used for trained fruit trees (Fig. 14). All of these are trained perfectly flat so they take up minimum space. Apples and pears can be grown as cordons, each consisting of a single stem furnished with fruiting spurs. The trees are planted at an angle of 45°. Apples and pears can also be grown as espaliers. Each consists of a central trunk supporting, at 45 cm (18 in) intervals, pairs of horizontal branches furnished with fruiting spurs. Peaches, cherries and plums can be grown as fans. A fan has a very short trunk, from the top of which branches spread out in a fan shape. Each branch produces side shoots on which the fruits are carried.

Fruits should be given plenty of sun and remember that with some, particularly apples and pears, several varieties are needed (all with the same flowering period) to ensure fertilization of the flowers and hence good crops of fruits. A garden centre supplying fruits should be able to advise on this aspect of fruit growing and ensure you choose suitable varieties.

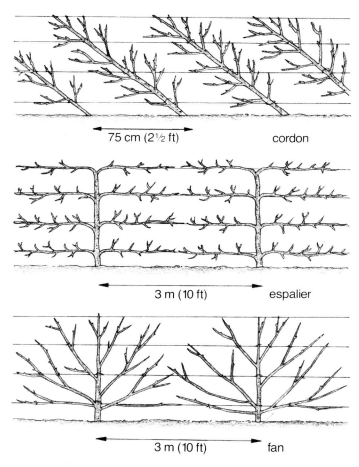

75 cm (2½ ft)   cordon

3 m (10 ft)   espalier

3 m (10 ft)   fan

Fig. 14 Trained fruit trees like cordons, espaliers and fans make an attractive and highly productive screen for a vegetable plot. They are supported with a system of posts and wires.

Another way of attractively screening a vegetable plot is to grow a hedge around it. A range of hedging plants is described in Chapter 1. When screening a vegetable plot try to make sure the screen does not cast shade for long periods over the plot as the majority of vegetables need plenty of sun.

OLD TREES AND TREE STUMPS

Big old trees and tall tree stumps can be hidden or made more attractive by growing climbing plants up them. Very large trees will need vigorous, very tall climbers, and there are certainly plenty of these available. There are also smaller climbers suitable for stumps and smaller trees (such as old unproductive apple trees).

Plant the climber 30–45 cm (12–18 in) away from the trunk of the tree and initially guide it up the trunk with bamboo canes. Once it reaches the branches it will support itself.

CHOICE OF CLIMBERS
Celastrus orbiculatus (staff vine) This has already been described on page 45.

Clematis montana (mountain clematis) Produces a profusion of white flowers in spring; also pink-flowered varieties; deciduous; takes sun or shade; extremely vigorous, attaining 12 m (40 ft) in height.

Clematis tangutica (clematis) A delightful smaller late summer/autumn flowering species with yellow blooms; deciduous; likes plenty of sun; height 6 m (20 ft).

Lonicera × americana (honeysuckle) This has fragrant flowers in the summer – they start white but then turn yellow; deciduous; likes a sunny spot; height 9 m (30 ft).

Polygonum baldschuanicum (Russian vine) This has already been described on page 48.

Roses There are several climbing and rambler roses which can be grown up trees and tall tree stumps. Very vigorous is 'Félicité et Perpétue', a rambler with large clusters of cream blooms, height 5.4 m (18 ft). Also for very large trees is *Rosa filipes* 'Kiftsgate', a climber with masses of small white flowers in mid-summer; height 9 m (30 ft).

Rosa longicuspis also has small white flowers in profusion; height at least 6 m (20 ft). The vigorous rambler, 'Rambling Rector', has double white flowers in mid-summer and can reach a height of at least 6 m (20 ft). 'The Garland' has highly scented semi-double creamy-white blooms in early and mid-summer and can reach a height of about 4.5 m (15 ft). For something really different try 'Veilchenblau' with small semi-double violet-purple blooms; tolerates shade; height around 4.5 m (15 ft). The rambler 'Wedding Day' has very fragrant single pale yellowish white blooms in summer; height 7.6 m (25 ft).

Schizophragma hydrangeoides Heads of creamy-white flowers in summer; deciduous; plenty of sun needed; height up to 9 m (30 ft).

Vitis coignetiae (Japanese crimson glory vine) Huge leaves which take on stunning autumn tints; deciduous; plenty of sun needed; extremely vigorous, capable of reaching a height of 27 m (90 ft).

SERVICES INSPECTION COVERS

Inspection covers for underground services (amusingly known as man-hole covers in the UK) are invariably on full view (often where we want to lay a lawn or build a patio. Fortunately there are a couple of very good ways of hiding them.

It is possible to buy from garden centres ornamental concrete plant containers which fit perfectly over inspection covers–presumably they are made specially for the purpose (Fig. 15a). From experience I know that they are extremely heavy and there is always the possibility that they will have to be moved if anything goes wrong with the underground services.

You might consider making your own container out of timber, which would be much lighter. It should be at least 30 cm (12 in) deep to prevent rapid drying out of compost in warm weather and to give plants a sufficiently deep root run.

The container is filled with good potting compost, ideally a lightweight soilless type to avoid excessive

Fig. 15a An ornamental concrete plant container chosen to fit exactly over an inspection cover. It contains a collection of dwarf conifers which give year-round colour and interest.

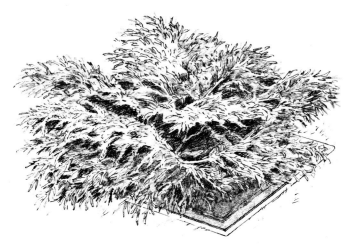

Fig. 15b A prostrate juniper, *Juniperus communis* 'Repanda', with dense mats of deep green foliage, tinted bronze in winter, effectively hiding an inspection cover.

weight (bearing in mind that the container may have to be moved). Then you can fill the container with plants of your choice–perhaps colourful spring and summer bedding plants, or with dwarf conifers or other diminutive shrubs. It would also look good planted with a collection of alpines provided it receives plenty of sun.

Another idea for hiding an inspection cover is to plant a prostrate juniper (Fig. 15b) or cotoneaster alongside it, which will then spread over the cover. Make sure you position the plant so that the leading shoot is pointing towards the centre of the cover. For a very quick effect you could even plant two, one on each side of the cover.

Varieties of the creeping juniper, *Juniperus horizontalis*, are ideal for the purpose, especially the more vigorous kinds like 'Bar Harbor' with grey-blue foliage, which becomes flushed with mauve in winter; 'Emerald Spreader', bright green foliage; 'Glauca'

with very dense foliage which is greyish blue in colour and at its most intense during the summer; and 'Hughes' with well-textured silvery foliage.

I can also recommend other prostrate junipers like *J. communis* 'Repanda' with dense mats of deep green foliage which, in winter, becomes tinted with bronze; *J. sabina tamariscifolia* with greyish blue well-textured foliage; and *J. squamata* 'Blue Carpet' which forms a sheet of vivid silvery-blue foliage. All of the junipers are evergreen so will give year-round effect.

Evergreen prostrate cotoneasters would also be suitable for hiding an inspection cover and are noted for their crops of red or orange berries in the autumn. Try *C. salicifolius* varieties 'Parkteppich' or 'Repens'; *C.* 'Skogholm'; or *C. dammeri radicans*.

Fig. 16 A prefabricated raised swimming pool effectively landscaped into the surroundings by means of raised timber decking, timber steps and dense planting. Lush large-leaved foliage plants would create a pleasing effect, such as phormiums, ornamental grasses, *Fatsia japonica* and ivies. Don't plant them too close to the pool.

All the plants described above can have their stems lifted up and tied back out of the way if it becomes necessary to gain access to the inspection cover. This will not damage the plants – carried out carefully.

THE RAISED SWIMMING POOL

A prefabricated raised swimming pool can provide a good deal of fun for a modest outlay but it cannot be considered an object of beauty, and it certainly does not blend into the garden unless serious thought is given to landscaping the surrounds.

One way of hiding the pool and turning it into an attractive feature is shown in Fig. 16. Here half of the pool is hidden with raised timber decking which, of course, makes an ideal area for sitting and all the general activities associated with aquatic entertainment. Ideally the decking is built in front of a wall – perhaps this would be a solution to the problem of that unsightly garage wall. Timber steps, with open risers, are comparatively simple to make and give access to the decking, at the same time hiding yet more of the pool.

The remaining part of the pool could be hidden by grouping plants around it, but do not plant them too close for if water is splashed on them they may be damaged or killed, due to the chemicals which are added to swimming-pool water. Lush, large-leaved foliage plants would create a pleasing effect, such as phormiums, ornamental grasses, *Fatsia japonica* and ivies.

If you do not want to make the timber decking too high then the pool could be partially sunk into the ground, excavating a circle with a greater diameter than that of the pool to avoid having soil right up to the sides.

A Japanese-style garden is especially recommended for small town and city gardens, providing a tranquil retreat.

Water is often featured in Japanese gardens and invariably a bridge is constructed over a pool.

5

CHANGING THE ENVIRONMENT

With appropriate planning and planting of the garden, your house can be set in an atmosphere which is completely different from the locality. A garden can make you feel that you are in the Mediterranean, even if the climate is cool; that you are in the country, even though you live in the centre of town; that you are in a tropical climate; or it can even provide the peace and tranquility of a Japanese garden.

Colour schemes can be used to create feelings of warmth or coolness, depending on the climate. All of these aspects of creating illusions in gardens are considered here.

A MEDITERRANEAN GARDEN

A warm sunny garden with very well-drained soil could be turned into a little bit of the Mediterranean countryside. As many of the most appropriate plants are not the hardiest of subjects, this type of garden is best suited to milder climates. The idea can be specially recommended for mild seaside gardens.

Anyone who has visited Mediterranean countries such as Spain, the South of France, Italy and the adjacent islands, Greece and its islands, Turkey and the north coast of Africa will know that much of the terrain is very rocky and rugged. This effect could quite easily be created in a garden with some low but bold outcrops of natural rock and the planting areas covered with stone chippings or rock fragments. Even paths, winding between the rock outcrops, could be formed of chippings. Keep the design as natural-looking and as rugged as possible.

Shrubs, perennials and bulbs are then planted between and around the rock outcrops. Space permitting, a few specimen trees could be used here and there as focal points and to give height to the planting scheme. Pines and cypresses would be the most appropriate trees, choosing those which are found in the Mediterranean, like the Italian or Mediterranean cypress, *Cupressus sempervirens*, which forms a narrow deep green column about 7.6 m (25 ft) high after about 20 years. Appropriate pines are *Pinus pinea*, the stone pine or umbrella pine, with a dome-shaped crown densely furnished with deep green needles, height and spread after 20 years at least 6 m (20 ft); and *P. pinaster*, the maritime pine, a very fast grower with a tall domed crown and stiff, light green needles, the height after 20 years being about 14 m (45 ft) and the spread 6 m (20 ft). Both of these pines are ideal for coastal gardens and poor sandy soils.

It is sensible to choose other plants, too, which are native to or found in Mediterranean countries. I can particularly recommend the following.

Shrubs

Cercis siliquastrum (Judas tree) Pink-purple flowers profusely borne on bare twigs in spring; deciduous; height and spread over 4.5 m (15 ft).

Cistus (sun rose) There are several suitable species of these dwarf or medium height compact evergreen shrubs which bear single-rose-like flowers in spring and early summer. Try *C. ladanifer*, the gum cistus, with white flowers blotched with brown; *C. populifolius*, white flowers, blotched yellow; and *C. × skanbergii*, a wild hybrid with pink blooms.

Colutea arborescens (bladder senna) Produces yellow pea-like flowers all through summer, followed by fat seed pods; deciduous pinnate foliage; height and spread about 2.4 m (8 ft).

Coronilla emerus (scorpion senna) Succession of bright yellow pea flowers in summer; deciduous pinnate foliage; height and spread 1.8 m (6 ft).

Cytisus (broom) These shrubs produce masses of pea-shaped flowers in spring or early summer. Suitable species include *C. albus*, white flowers, height and spread 1.8 m (6 ft); *C. battandieri*, deep yellow flowers with fruity scent, height and spread about 3.6 m (12 ft); and *C. purgans*, deep yellow scented flowers, height and spread 1.2 m (4 ft).

Erica arborea (tree heath) Sprays of white flowers in spring; evergreen; height 3.6 m (12 ft), spread 2.4 m (8 ft). Needs acid soil.

Genista (broom) The brooms produce pea-like flowers in spring or summer. There are several suitable species for the Mediterranean garden, including: *G. aetnensis* The Mount Etna broom, with deep yellow flowers, height and spread at least 4.5 m (15 ft); *G. cinerea*, fragrant yellow flowers, height and spread about 2.4 m (8 ft); and *G. hispanica*, the Spanish gorse, a very prickly dense shrub with deep yellow flowers, height and spread about 1.2 m (4 ft).

Halimium ocymoides Yellow, brown-blotched, single-rose-like flowers in early summer; evergreen greyish foliage; height and spread about 90 cm (3 ft).

Helianthemum (rock rose) Excellent prostrate evergreen shrubs for hot dry spots, especially for scrambling over rocks. They flower prolifically in summer. Species include the yellow *H. alpestre* with grey-green foliage and *H. lunulatum*, also with greyish foliage and yellow flowers.

Laurus nobilis (sweet bay) Famed for its aromatic evergreen foliage which is used for flavouring all kinds of food. Height and spread at least 4.5 m (15 ft) but can be restricted by judicious pruning in spring.

Lavandula stoechas (French lavender) Produces spikes of purple flowers in late spring and summer; aromatic evergreen foliage, greyish green; height and spread 60 cm (2 ft).

Phlomis fruticosa (Jerusalem sage) Produces yellow flowers, in whorls around the stems, during summer; evergreen leaves, hairy and greyish green; height up to 1.2 m (4 ft), spread 60 cm (2 ft).

Rosmarinus officinalis (rosemary) A popular shrub with deep green, aromatic, evergreen foliage and blue flowers in spring and summer; height and spread about 1.8 m (6 ft).

Spartium junceum (Spanish broom) Green rush-like stems bear deep yellow pea-shaped flowers in summer; height and spread at least 2.4 m (8 ft).

Perennials

Centranthus ruber (red valerian) Clusters of deep pink flowers throughout summer; bluish grey foliage; height up to 90 cm (3 ft), spread 30 cm (1 ft).

Echinops ritro (globe thistle) A somewhat thistle-like plant with globular heads of metallic-blue flowers in summer and greyish foliage; height up to 1.2 m (4 ft), spread 60 cm (2 ft).

Euphorbia (spurge) Several species would be suitable for the Mediterranean garden, including *E. characias*, acid-yellow flower heads in spring and early summer; evergreen grey leaves; height and spread about 90 cm (3 ft). Try also *E. myrsinites* with acid-yellow flower heads in spring; evergreen grey foliage; height 15 cm (6 in), spread 45 cm (18 in). Well worth growing is *E. wulfenii*, with large heads of greeny yellow flowers in summer; evergreen grey foliage; height and spread 1.2 m (4 ft).

Helleborus foetidus (stinking hellebore) Green bowl-shaped flowers are produced in spring; foliage evergreen, dark green, with a strong smell when bruised; height and spread 60 cm (2 ft).

This cottage-style garden is, surprisingly, in the middle of town, providing a 'country retreat' for its owner.

A typically English cottage garden full of summer flowers: yet it is located in a town.

Iris unguicularis (Algerian iris) A winter-flowering iris with blue flowers; grassy evergreen foliage; height 20 cm (8 in), spread 45 cm (18 in).

Bulbs

There is a wealth of small and miniature bulbs which come from the Mediterranean region and well worth drifting around the shrubs and perennials. Choose species of allium (ornamental onion), colchicum (autumn crocus), crocus, hardy cyclamen, fritillaria (fritillary), *Leucojum autumnale* (autumn snowflake), *Lilium candidum* (madonna lily), narcissus (miniature daffodils like *N. bulbocodium* and *N. cyclamineus*), ornithogalum (star of Bethlehem), scilla (squill), *Sternbergia lutea* and tulipa (tulip species like *T. clusiana*, *T. sylvestris* and *T. praecox*).

A COTTAGE GARDEN

The cottage-style garden is enjoying a revival. Surprisingly, perhaps, many owners of small town gardens are creating cottage gardens and very good they look, too, in such an unlikely environment. And why shouldn't the town dweller try to create the feeling that he or she lives in the country?

A cottage garden is typically an English style of gardening – traditionally a colourful mixture of all kinds of plants, generally grown in straight borders on each side of a central path leading from the gate to the front door. Often this was an old brick path, partially covered by sprawling plants at the front of the borders. If you want to make use of this idea, then do make the path extra wide to allow for plants spreading on to it.

Traditionally vegetables are grown among the flowers, which include old-fashioned perennials, annuals, bulbs, shrubs and climbers – especially honeysuckle and roses around the front door. An apple

tree or two provide shade and fruit, while another typical cottage-garden fruit tree is the black mulberry, *Morus nigra*.

Intensively planted borders need a fair amount of maintenance due to the wide variety of plants grown and, of course, plants have to be kept under control by regular lifting and dividing, pruning back and so on, to ensure they do not encroach on their neighbours.

The permanent 'framework' of the borders can be provided by old-fashioned shrubs like philadelphus (mock orange); *Syringa vulgaris* (lilac); *Chaenomeles japonica* (ornamental quince); *Daphne mezereum* (mezereon); *Ribes sanguineum* (flowering currant); *Buddleia davidii* (butterfly bush); forsythias; and, of course, old-fashioned shrub roses, like the moss roses.

Climbers can include *Lonicera periclymenum* varieties (honeysuckle); climbing and rambler roses; *Jasminum officinale* (summer jasmine); *Jasminum nudiflorum* (winter jasmine); *Clematis montana* varieties and *C. alpina*; *Vitis* 'Brant' (grape vine); and *Hedera helix* varieties (ivy).

There is a wide range of old-fashioned perennials that can be planted among the shrubs, like *Aconitum napellus* (monkshood); *Althaea rosea* (hollyhock); aquilegia (columbine); artemisias like the grey-leaved 'Lambrook Silver'; asters (Michaelmas daisies); aubrieta for trailing over the edge of the path; dwarf campanulas (bellflowers) for the same purpose; delphiniums; dianthus (border pinks and carnations); digitalis (foxgloves); *Helleborus niger* (Christmas rose); *Iris unguicularis* (Algerian or winter-flowering iris); lupins; paeonia (peony); kniphofias (red-hot pokers); nepeta (catmint) ideal for the edge of the border; primulas or coloured primroses; *Sidalcea malviflora* varieties; verbascum (mullein); and viola (violets).

Old-fashioned hardy annuals can be sown in any gaps in the spring, like nigella (love-in-a-mist); calendula (pot marigold); iberis (candytuft); matthiola (stocks); centaurea (cornflower); and *Salvia sclarea* (clary). Half-hardy annuals suitable for cottage-garden borders include nicotiana (flowering tobacco); pelargoniums (geraniums); verbena (vervain); and heliotropium (heliotrope).

There is a wide range of spring-flowering bulbs, particularly dwarf kinds like crocuses, galanthus (snowdrops), muscari (grape hyacinths), scillas (squills) and dwarf tulip species.

Include some of the more attractive and popular wild flowers, too, which in Britain could include *Primula vulgaris* (primrose); *Primula veris* (cowslip); *Chrysanthemum leucanthemum* (ox-eye daisy); *Viola tricolor* (heartsease); and *Meconopsis cambrica* (Welsh poppy). All of these can be raised from seeds obtained from seedsmen who specialise in wild flowers.

The boundaries of the garden should ideally be enclosed with a natural or country hedge, as described under 'Preserving Pleasant Views', in Chapter 3.

Bush fruits such as currants and gooseberries are traditionally grown in the borders, together with vegetables. For instance, runner beans, which are very colourful when in flower, could be grown up a wig-wam of sticks or canes at the back of a border; and the more attractive salad crops and small vegetables, like lettuces, spring onions, beetroots, carrots, endive and bush tomatoes, could be grown in groups at the front. Herbs of all kinds will look completely at home in the border. In the past, they were widely grown by cottagers.

A TAME JUNGLE

An idea for a town or city garden, perhaps surrounded by high buildings, is to turn it into a lush, jungle-like garden, densely planted with mainly evergreens, especially large-leaved kinds, and exotic-looking climbers.

Several city gardeners I know have used this idea and have found that it creates an exotic oasis, blotting out the surrounding 'landscape' and muffling outside noise. Winding paths weave between the plants, leading to secret, very secluded areas. The boundaries in particular are very densely planted, especially with tall climbing plants.

Evergreen shrubs

Choose exotic-looking shrubs such as plenty of large-leaved kinds. I have already described a good selection in Chapter 1 – aucuba, eriobotrya, fatsia, *Magnolia grandiflora*, *Mahonia japonica*, trachycarpus and *Viburnum rhytidophyllum*. Other exotic-looking evergreens I can recommend are described below.

Acacia (wattle) Only suitable for growing outdoors in mild areas, needing full sun, protection from wind and acid soil. Yellow flowers in winter or spring. Recommended species are *A. baileyana*, *A. dealbata* and *A. mucronata*, all becoming large shrubs.

Bamboo There are several genera to choose from, like arundinaria. Popular species here are *A. japonica*, *A. murielae*, *A. nitida* and *A. viridistriata*, all of which grow quite tall. Phyllostachys has some graceful tall species like *P. bambusoides*, *P. flexuosa* and *P. nigra* 'Boryana'. A large, broad-leaved bamboo is *Sasa tessellata*. Bamboos like moisture-retentive soil, shelter from cold winds and will thrive in sun or partial shade.

Callistemon (bottle brush) Half-hardy Australian shrubs, only suitable for mild areas, with bottle-brush-like flowers, scarlet in *C. citrinus* 'Splendens' and light yellow in *C. salignus*. They need full sun.

Crinodendron hookeranum Again, only for mild areas. Produces red lantern-like flowers in spring/early summer. Height and spread at least 3 m (10 ft). Acid soil in partial shade.

Desfontainea spinosa Recommended for all but very cold areas. Holly-like leaves and tubular red and yellow flowers in summer. Height and spread at least 1.8 m (6 ft). Acid soil and partial shade.

Embothrium coccineum lanceolatum (Chilean fire bush) Only for mild areas. Vivid orange-red flowers in spring/early summer. Acid soil and full sun or partial shade. Height over 6 m (20 ft), spread 3 m.

Eucalyptus (gum trees) These can be grown as shrubs if they are pruned hard each spring. Several species can be grown outdoors like *E. gunnii* and *E. niphophila*. Full sun and shelter, moisture-retentive yet well-drained soil.

A lush, jungle–like garden in London, densely planted with mainly foliage plants: truly an exotic oasis.

This jungle-like London garden, featuring large-leaved foliage plants, blots out the surrounding 'landscape' and muffles outside noise.

Grevillea Australian shrubs, only suited to outdoor cultivation in mild areas. Species available: *G. alpina*, dwarf habit, red and yellow flowers; *G. rosmarinifolia*, deep red flowers, height and spread 1.8 m (6 ft); and *G. sulphurea*, yellow flowers, of similar size. Acid soil, full sun and shelter.

Leptospermum scoparium Australian and New Zealand shrub with masses of white, pink or red flowers in spring and early summer. There are numerous varieties. Height and spread at least 1.8 m (6 ft). Acid or neutral soil, full sun and shelter.

Pittosporum Foliage shrubs for mild areas. Best-known is *P. tenuifolium* with light green foliage, and its varieties, some of which are variegated. Height at least 4.5 m (15 ft), spread 2.4 m (8 ft). *P. tobira* has whorls of large bright green leaves, height and spread 3 m (10 ft). Well-drained soil in full sun, sheltered from cold winds.

Sophora tetraptera (Kowhai, New Zealand laburnum) Clusters of tubular yellow flowers in late spring, pinnate foliage; height at least 6 m (20 ft), spread 3 m (10 ft). Well-drained soil, full sun and shelter.

Telopea truncata (Tasmanian waratah) Spectacular deep red spidery flower heads in early summer and large thick-textured leaves; height in excess of 3 m (10 ft); acid moisture-retentive yet well-drained soil, partial shade, shelter.

Exotic climbers and wall shrubs

These all require a warm sunny wall well sheltered from cold winds. The protection afforded by an enclosed town or city garden should ensure success but outdoor cultivation in very cold parts of the country would be risky.

Abutilon Evergreen wall shrubs with bell or bowl-shaped flowers in summer. Best-known is *A. megapotamicum*, red and yellow flowers, height and spread at least 2.4 m (8 ft). Of similar stature is *A.* × *suntense* 'Jermyns' with deep mauve flowers, and *A. vitifolium*, also with mauve flowers.

Aristolochia macrophylla (Dutchman's pipe) A vigorous deciduous climber to at least 6 m (20 ft) bearing, in early summer, pipe-shaped yellowish-green blooms.

Campsis radicans (trumpet vine) Deciduous climber to 12 m (40 ft), producing large red and orange trumpet-shaped flowers in late summer/early autumn.

Clianthus puniceus (lobster's claw) A semi-evergreen wall shrub with ferny foliage and brilliant red lobster-claw-like flowers in early summer; height up to 3.6 m (12 ft).

Doxantha (Bignonia) capreolata Evergreen climber to 12 m (40 ft), with tubular yellow-red flowers in summer.

Eccremocarpus scaber (Chilean glory flower) Half-hardy climber with ferny foliage and clusters of scarlet or orange tubular flowers in summer and autumn. Height 3–4 m (10–12 ft). Protect base of plant in winter with bracken or straw.

Fremontodendron (Fremontia) californicum Semi-evergreen or deciduous wall shrub with large deep yellow bowl-shaped flowers in summer. Height about 3.6 m (12 ft). *F.* 'California Glory' is also worth looking out for.

Jasminum mesnyi (J. primulinum) (primrose jasmine) Evergreen climber to 3 m (10 ft), with yellow flowers in spring.

Lapageria rosea (Chilean bell-flower) An evergreen climber with large pinky-red bell-shaped flowers in summer and early autumn. Can attain 4.5 m (15 ft) in height. Acid soil, moisture-retentive yet well drained, humus-rich; best in partial shade.

Mandevilla suaveolens (Chilean jasmine) A deciduous climber to 5 m (16 ft) with highly scented white starry flowers in summer.

Passiflora caerulea (blue passion flower) Vigorous evergreen climber to at least 6 m (20 ft), with very exotic-looking blue and white flowers in summer and early autumn, sometimes followed by orange-yellow fruits.

Tecomaria capensis Evergreen climber to 4.5 m (15 ft) with pinnate foliage and long tubular orange-scarlet flowers in late summer.

A JAPANESE-STYLE GARDEN

If you want to create an oriental atmosphere then consider a Japanese-style garden. The idea is especially recommended for small town and city gardens.

The design and planting should be simple (it is a great mistake to overcrowd a Japanese garden) and should aim to create a tranquil atmosphere. One can never create a true Japanese garden outside of Japan (for instance the climate and light intensity are often not quite suitable and it may not be possible to match construction materials exactly) but nevertheless one can create a perfectly acceptable Japanese-style garden.

The style which consists purely of areas of raked sand and rocks is not what I have in mind but rather a garden which contains several pleasing features and a reasonably good selection of plants.

Space is very important and this could be provided by an area of gravel which could be used for sitting and walking, perhaps with stepping stones winding through it to some other part of the garden. Some groups of natural well-shaped rocks, set in pebbles or sand, could act as focal points in the garden. Do not use white limestone rocks, though, as they are too glaring. Always use a combination of tall dramatic rocks and others that are lower and flatter, which can be partially buried in the ground.

Slightly raised beds for plants will give variation in height and these can be planted with pleasing specimen plants. Secret areas can be created by screening parts of the garden with bamboo screens (rather like trelliswork), made from thick bamboo poles. A pergola could also be formed from bamboo. Climbing plants can be grown on both – what better than the Japanese wisteria, *W. floribunda*?

Water is often featured in Japanese gardens and pools are very informal. Often a bridge is constructed over a pool, at its simplest a large stone slab; or stepping stones are provided. A specimen tree by the pool, such as a small pine, will give height to this feature.

Do not be tempted to have too many ornaments. Certainly one or two Japanese (or Japanese style) stone lanterns would further help to create the right atmosphere, positioning them where light is actually needed, and using candles to provide the light. Often a Japanese maple is grown by a lantern and allowed to arch over it.

The Japanese also try to create the illusion of depth in their gardens, often by planting a large tree in the foreground and a smaller tree some distance behind it. The large tree is kept thinned so that the crown is not too dense and so that the small tree can be seen through the branches. Also used is the technique of planting large-leaved shrubs in the foreground and small-leaved kinds behind them.

I have already mentioned that one should use plants with restaint and not overcrowd the garden. Instead rely on shapely or distinctive specimen plants. Restrained use of colour is also characteristic of Japanese gardens: green being the main colour. Colour is very often used to herald the seasons: for instance, an ornamental cherry tree might denote that spring has arrived; an azalea that early summer is here; and a maple with brilliant foliage tints used to announce the arrival of autumn. All of these plants need a dark background, such as deep green shrubs to show up the flowers or foliage.

A choice of plants

The Japanese maple, *Acer palmatum*, is invaluable for its autumn leaf colour. It is a small rounded tree, very slow growing, with an eventual height and spread of about 6 m (20 ft).

Bamboos are very much a part of Japanese gardens, and descriptions of a good range will be found on page 65. A camellia can be grown to herald the spring, ideally a variety of *Camellia japonica* (native to Japan). Remember camellias need acid soil and protection from early morning sun. Height and spread can be up to 3.6 m (12 ft).

Spring could also be welcomed with one of the

Different levels in a garden, whether natural or artificial, should ideally be linked with steps, to encourage visitors to explore.

One of the easiest ways of creating a variation in level is to build a multi-level patio.

Japanese magnolias: *M. liliiflora*, conical reddish purple flowers, height and spread in excess of 2.4 m (8 ft); *M. salicifolia*, white starry flowers, height 6 m (20 ft), spread 3 m (10 ft); and *M. stellata*, also with white starry flowers, height and spread about 3 m (10 ft). All are deciduous.

Japanese pines are appropriate trees, including the Japanese black pine, *Pinus thunbergii*, of conical habit to a height of about 22 m (75 ft). The Japanese red pine, *P. densiflora*, can attain a similar height; it has reddish bark and is conical when young but eventually becomes flat-topped. Both are suitable only for large gardens. For smaller gardens I can recommend *P. densiflora* 'Umbraculifera', with an ultimate height and spread of 3 m (10 ft). It is a slow grower and somewhat mushroom-shaped. *P. densiflora* and its variety will not grow in chalky soils.

A small flowering tree could well be one of the prunus, such as the Yoshino cherry, *Prunus × yedoensis*, with a graceful arching habit of growth and white scented flowers in early spring; height and spread about 7.6 m (25 ft). *Prunus mume* is the Japanese apricot with scented pink flowers in late winter/early spring; height and spread up to 7.6 m (25 ft). The weeping spring cherry, *P. subhirtella* 'Pendula Rosea', can also be recommended, with pale pink flowers in early to mid-spring; height and spread up to 4.5 m (15 ft). For autumn and winter flowers there is the autumn cherry, *P. subhirtella* 'Autumnalis', with white flowers; height and spread up to 9 m (30 ft).

Evergreen hybrid azaleas flower during mid- to late spring and are dwarf spreading shrubs, generally 1–1.2 m (3–4 ft) in height with a similar spread. The Kurume hybrids are probably the best known and include such popular varieties as 'Hinodegiri' in brilliant crimson and 'Hinomayo' in purest pink. These azaleas like dappled shade and need an acid or lime-free, cool moist soil.

A small weeping willow is *Salix matsudana* 'Pendula', but I would suggest that only owners of large gardens should consider it.

ATMOSPHERE WITH COLOUR

Colours can be used in gardens to create feelings of warmth or coolness – which mood you go for will probably depend on climate. Gardeners living in a cool climate will want to create the feeling of warmth, while those in warm climates will be striving for cool effects.

'Warm' colour schemes

To create the feeling of warmth you could use a red colour scheme, choosing plants with red flowers and foliage. You could also include purple, violet, red-violet, orange-red and orange. Bear in mind that a bed or border of plants in these colours could be rather overpowering, so don't overdo it.

A pink and silver planting scheme also creates a warm atmosphere, but is more subtle than a red scheme. Use a combination of pink-flowered plants and silver- or grey-leaved plants.

A yellow scheme creates a cheerful 'sunny' atmosphere. You could also include plants with cream flowers or foliage, plus some plants with grey foliage.

'Cool' colour schemes

A white and green scheme will create a cool atmosphere, using plants with white as well as green flowers. Use plenty of foliage plants, too, especially white-variegated kinds.

A blue scheme can also be recommended for creating a cool atmosphere, using blue-flowered plants, but including some with white or cream blooms. Again use a good quantity of foliage plants, choosing those with bluish or greyish foliage.

6

UPS AND DOWNS

The majority of gardens, particularly small town and suburban plots, are perfectly flat, yet there is no need for them to appear to be so for it is an easy matter to create different levels. This, of course, makes for a more interesting garden.

RAISED PATIOS

One of the easiest ways of creating a variation in level is to have a raised patio or sitting area. One point to bear in mind at the outset, however, is that if the patio is to butt against a wall of the house, do make sure the level is not above the damp-proof course otherwise you will have serious problems from rising damp. If this is unavoidable, then build it against a boundary wall if you have one.

I am not necessarily advocating building to a great height – indeed, a height of between 15 and 30 cm (6 and 12 in) is often sufficient to give a pleasing effect.

Building a raised patio does not entail much more work than laying a patio on the flat. The edges can be formed of dwarf walls, built with bricks, ornamental concrete walling blocks or utility concrete building blocks. Then you will have to fill in, almost up to the top of the walls, with rubble, which you will no doubt have to buy in, perhaps from a building or demolition firm, but it should be cheap enough. The well-firmed rubble is then covered with a layer of builders' sand to create a smooth level surface and then paving slabs are laid in the normal way.

If you want to go higher then I suggest a multi-level patio. Fig. 17a shows a two-level corner patio which would make an attractive feature in any garden. The second level is simply built on top of the first.

Or you might prefer a step-like patio as shown in Fig. 17b. This is like a very wide flight of steps, which could lead to a boundary wall, perhaps with an arched mirror to create the illusion of extra depth. This patio, of course, would entail a good deal of brickwork and lots of rubble to build up to a reasonable height. I would suggest dense evergreen planting on each side of this patio to camouflage the walls. Each level need only be about 15 cm (6 in) higher than the preceding one. To create an illusion of depth, this patio could be tapered from the front to the back – in other words, make it much wider at the front than at the back. This is clearly shown in the drawing.

TIMBER DECKING

Timber decking provides a comparatively easy means of constructing a raised sitting area as it is usually a low structure built on stout timber piles.

It is more widely used in America than in the UK, although it is catching on in this country and indeed one can buy ready-made units. Decking can, of course, be stained any natural wood colour, from dark oak to chestnut or western red cedar, to blend in with the surroundings.

Timber steps can be built for easy access, ideally with open risers.

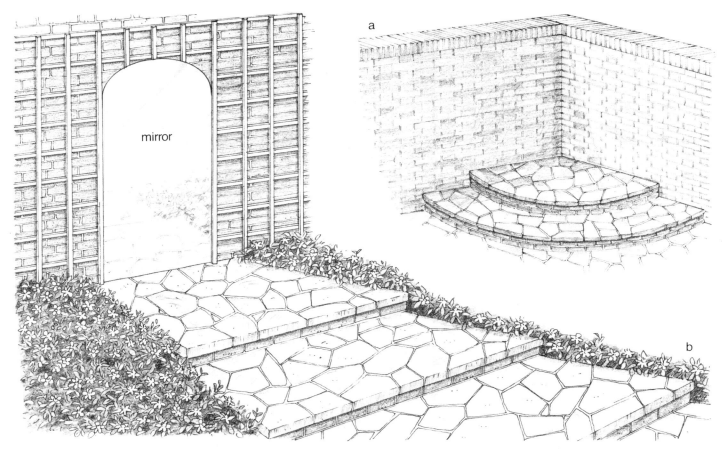

Fig. 17a A two-level corner patio would make an attractive feature in any garden: an easy way of creating different levels in flat plots.

Fig. 17b A step-like patio, rather like a wide flight of steps, creates variation in levels in this otherwise flat garden. It tapers from front to back to create an illusion of depth.

STEPS

One should incorporate steps into the design of a garden wherever possible to link the different levels. A flight of steps can be a feature in its own right – and do not think that they have to lead anywhere. Why not consider a flight of steps leading up to a suitable wall mural, such as a view through an archway?

Soil could be built up on each side of this flight of steps to form a bank and, of course, this will mean buying in topsoil from a local supplier. This bank could then be densely planted with dwarf and low-growing plants with a ground-covering habit of growth. Again, never construct such a feature above the damp-proof course of house walls.

Suitable plants for clothing banks include ivies, prostrate junipers, vincas and *Hypericum calycinum*.

Timber decking provides a comparatively easy means of constructing a raised sitting area and can be coloured to match surroundings.

RAISED BORDERS

Why not consider having slightly raised borders in the garden? These create variation in levels and are certainly not difficult to build. I much prefer raised borders to having raised beds (which tend to look like billiard tables) dotted around the garden.

The borders need not be too high – a maximum of 30 cm 12 in) generally creates sufficient variation in level. Make them reasonably wide if the size of garden allows – not narrow strips which are difficult to plant effectively.

Borders can be built up in a variety of ways. In a country or natural setting you might like to use sections of tree trunk held in place with wooden stakes. Or, if you can obtain them, timber railway sleepers are ideal and will last a life-time. In Britain one can now buy artificial timber sleepers for building raised borders.

Bricks can also be used to build up the borders, and should be matched, if possible, with the house bricks. Or you might prefer ornamental concrete walling blocks which resemble natural stone. Natural stone walling is probably the most expensive material and aesthetically it is highly pleasing in any situation. It can, of course, be dry-laid.

When you have built the walls you will need to fill the borders with good-quality topsoil. This may be an opportunity to change the soil type in your garden. For instance, if you are on alkaline soil and want to grow lime-hating plants, then fill the borders with acid topsoil. In this instance, do make sure the borders are sufficiently deep – at least 30 cm (12 in).

Raised borders can, of course, be planted with whatever plants you desire and they have the advantage that they make an ideal home for trailing plants. These can be planted at the front and allowed to trail over the low walls.

RAISED PLATFORMS

Another way of creating height in a flat garden is to build some raised platforms for potted plants. These could be stepped or tiered and densely furnished with plants so that they look virtually like banks. Ideally raised platforms should be constructed against a wall. They can be built of timber or, if you want a more permanent structure, from bricks or building blocks. These can support concrete paving slabs on which to stand pots of plants.

Evergreen trailing plants would be ideal for 'clothing' the platforms, such as ivies and periwinkles. Among them other plants of your choice could be grown. The advantage of growing in pots is that the display can be easily changed if one tires of it.

7

PRACTICALITIES

Having arrived at this chapter you will be well aware that this book is concerned principally with ideas and design, but some practical tips on construction of features and planting techniques will, I hope, also be welcome.

CONSTRUCTION

Trellis screens and fencing

Trellis screens and prefabricated timber fencing panels need adequate posts for support. Use 8 cm (3 in) square fencing posts, treated with horticultural timber preservative. These are easily erected using proprietary metal post supports which are inserted in the ground. They are available from most good garden centres.

If you prefer to concrete posts into the ground, take out a 76 cm (2½ ft) deep hole for each post and then place 15 cm (6 in) of hardcore in the bottom. Wedge the post upright in the centre of the hole and then fill to ground level with a slightly moist concrete mix – 1 part cement to 4 parts all-in aggregate.

The sequence of erecting trellis or fencing panels is first to insert a post at one end, then secure a panel to it, using 8 cm (3 in) galvanized nails. Then insert the next post and nail the panel to that. Fix the second panel to this post. Continue in this way (note that the panels are held *between* the posts).

Trellis cladding

Trellis which is to be used for covering walls, fences, sheds and so on should, if it is to be used as a support for climbers, be held an inch or two away from the wall or other support. A good way of achieving this is to use old cotton reels as spacers wherever the screws are inserted. It is always best to use brass screws for fixing trellis in case you ever have to remove it (brass screws do not rust). Expanding plastic wall plugs will be needed for the screws when fixing trellis to brick walls.

Walls

Walls must be built on a really firm foundation. First remove a trench and then fill it with well-rammed hardcore topped with concrete. The foundation must be wider than the wall and the width should equal at least the depth of the concrete. The depth of hardcore must be of the same depth as the concrete. For a wall over six courses of bricks high, take out a trench 50 cm (20 in) deep (this will have 25 cm (10 in) of hardcore and 25 cm of concrete). Use a concrete mix of 1 part cement and 5 parts all-in aggregate.

Screen-block walls

The blocks – 30 × 30 × 10 cm (12 × 12 × 4 in) – are built up in stack bond (one block is placed immediately above another). The wall is supported at 1.8–3 m (6–10 ft) intervals with piers formed of hollow concrete cubes which are known as pilasters. These have slots, into which the blocks are locked. Each pillar should have steel reinforcing rods through it, bedded into the concrete foundation. Fill the piers with concrete as building proceeds.

Brick walls

When building a brick wall it is the usual practice to first build up at each end and then to fill in the middle, where bricks can be cut if necessary. A suitable mortar consists of 1 part cement and 6 parts builders' sand. Press the mortar joints into a 'V' shape with a brick-laying trowel.

Low walls, up to 60 cm (2 ft) high can be one brick thick; if over this height they should be two bricks thick. Bricks must overlap to create a staggered bond. The stretcher bond is simplest, where bricks are laid end to end. For walls which are two bricks thick lay courses of 'stretchers' (bricks laid end to end), alternating with courses of headers (bricks laid across the width of the wall). It is recommended that garden walls have a damp-proof course of low-water absorption bricks – these can form the first two courses. All walls must be finished with suitable coping.

Patios and paths

These must also have substantial foundations. First level and firm the soil. Next, cover with a 10 cm (4 in) layer of well-rammed hardcore. Cover this with 4 cm (1½ in) of soft builders' sand. Concrete paving slabs are then laid on the sand, spot-bedded on mortar (1 part cement, 6 parts sand), five pads of mortar for each slab. Leave 6 mm (¼ in) joints between slabs and later grout them with mortar. When laying, gently tap down each slab to ensure it is level.

Bricks for patios or paths are best loosely laid (not on mortar). Lay them flat (not on edge) and leave 9 mm (⅜ in) joints, which should be filled with sand. Use special hard paving bricks for patios and paths.

Steps

Don't make these too steep. The risers or vertical parts should be 15 cm (6 in) high and the treads (the parts you walk on) should be between 30 and 45 cm (12 and 18 in) deep. Make steps at least 90 cm (3 ft) wide.

An easy and excellent method of building steps is to have brick risers and paving slab treads. If building into a bank, the shape of the steps is first cut out in the bank. The slabs are laid on well-rammed hardcore. If you are building the flight of steps on a flat site (say leading up to a wall mural) then you will have to build up behind each riser with hardcore (such as broken bricks and concrete).

Timber pergola

Use 10 × 5 cm (4 × 2 in) timber with a sawn finish. Timber uprights should be sunk at least 60 cm (2 ft) into the ground and ideally concreted in. They should be 2.4 m (8 ft) high and spaced 1.8–2.4 m (6–8 ft) apart. They are placed in pairs and each pair joined together at the top with a length of timber. Further timbers are then used lengthways to form a grid framework.

All timber must be thoroughly treated with a horticultural wood preservative (this will not harm climbing plants). Preservatives are available in several natural-wood colours, like red cedar or dark oak.

PLANTING

All planting should be done in weed-free ground, ideally double-dug (to two depths of the spade blade), especially for permanent subjects like trees, shrubs, conifers, climbers, hedges and hardy perennials.

Shrubs and conifers

Most will be purchased containerized from garden centres. Evergreen shrubs and conifers in containers can be planted in spring, summer or early autumn. Root-balled evergreen shrubs and conifers (those lifted from the nurseryman's field with a ball of soil around the roots, and wrapped with hessian) are planted in early to mid-autumn or mid- to late spring.

Bare-root deciduous shrubs (as lifted from the nurseryman's field) are planted between late autumn and early spring, while they are dormant. Containerized deciduous shrubs may be planted at any time, but not if the soil is frozen or very wet.

To plant a root-balled or containerized shrub or conifer, remove a hole a bit larger than the root-ball and of such a depth that after planting the top of the root-ball is only slightly below soil level. Centralize the plant in the hole and return fine soil around it, firming well with your heels.

The hole for bare-root plants must be sufficiently large to allow the roots to be spread out to their full extent. Plant to the same depth that the plant was growing in the field – this is indicated by a soil mark at the base of the stem. Centralize the plant in the hole then place some fine soil over the roots. Gently shake the plant up and down to work this soil well between the roots. Then gradually replace the rest of the soil, at the same time firming well by treading with your heels.

On poor soil use a proprietary planting mixture: add some to the soil in the bottom of the hole and to the soil which is to be returned around the plant. Never allow newly planted subjects to dry out – keep well watered in dry periods.

Climbers

These are planted as for shrubs and conifers, but remember that they must not be planted right up against their support, such as a wall or fence, where the soil can be extremely dry, inhibiting establishment of the new plants. Plant about 30 cm (12 in) away from the wall or fence and use bamboo canes, angled towards the support, to guide the stems towards it.

Trees

Basically these are planted in the same way as shrubs and conifers but they must be provided with a stake for the first year or two. This should be inserted in the planting hole before the tree is positioned. Use an 8 cm (3 in) diameter timber tree stake. Make sure you choose a suitable length, bearing in mind that it must be inserted 45–60 cm (18–24 in) into the ground, with the top only just below the lowest branch of the tree. Then plant the tree, with the trunk only about 2.5 cm (1 in) away from the stake. When planting is complete, secure the trunk to the stake with plastic buckle-type tree ties, with a plastic buffer between stake and trunk. Place one tie at the top of the stake and another about 30 cm (12 in) above ground level. You may need a third mid-way between the two, especially if the trunk needs straightening.

Hedges

The method of planting is the same as for shrubs and conifers, but the plants are set in a single row; or in a double staggered row if you want a really wide hedge. Average planting distance is 45 cm (18 in) for most subjects. But needing 60 cm (24 in) spacing are conifers and large vigorous subjects such as laurels.

Perennials

Best planting time for hardy perennials is early to mid-spring. Autumn planting is only recommended if the soil is extremely well drained. Container-grown plants need a hole only slightly larger than the root-ball. With bare-root plants take out a hole deep enough to allow the roots to dangle straight down to their full extent. In each instance, though, the crown of the plant (where the buds are situated) must be level with surrounding soil when planting is complete. Never cover these buds with soil.

INDEX